Cra b

porcelain, mole and coconut crabs, among others; all are closely related to Brachyura but sufficiently distinct to place in a different infraorder.

Brachyura includes nearly 7,000 species, grouped into over ninety families. The brachyuran crabs share many characteristics, including exoskeletons that are moulted for the animal to grow (even during larval stages), segmented bodies, stalked eyes, carapaces broader than they are long, and similar appendages and mandibles. In most crabs, the first pair of legs (the chelipeds) is used for feeding and the legs terminate in curved, two-part claws or pincers (the chela). While some crabs can and do walk forwards, the sideways gait common among them is one of their most recognizable features. The majority of brachyuran species live their lives in the world's oceans, but about 12 per cent live on land or in fresh water.

Anomura includes some 2,500 species, which may seem more morphologically diverse than their brachyuran relatives: that is, they vary a great deal in form. Those evolved into the most

Charlotte Seid, *Pacific Sand Crab (Emerita analoga)*, 2019, ink on paper.

Charlotte Seid, *Coconut Crab (Birgus latro)*, 2019, ink on paper.

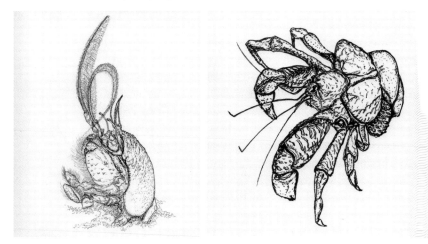

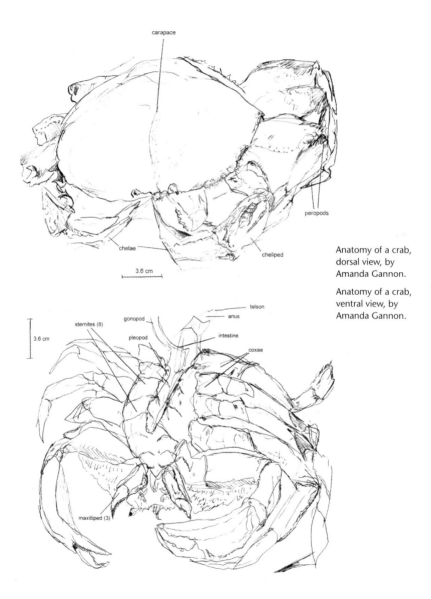

Anatomy of a crab, dorsal view, by Amanda Gannon.

Anatomy of a crab, ventral view, by Amanda Gannon.

crab-like forms (king, porcelain, hairy stone crabs and coconut crabs, for instance) are said to be carcinized. Still, they differ significantly from brachyurans – and from each other. Whereas 'Brachyura' translates from the Greek as 'short-tailed', 'Anomura' means differently tailed.[1] In both groups, 'tail' refers to the abdomen, which in true crabs is tucked compactly under the main body. In Anomura the abdomen can be elongated and curled, as in the squat lobster, or asymmetrical, as in the hermit crab. Many anomurans appear to have only eight limbs because a fifth pair of legs, smaller than the walking legs, are held inside the gill chambers and used for cleaning. Many of the 1,100 species of hermit crabs appear to have only six legs, since two pairs are not used for walking but rather squeezed into appropriated shells. Some anomurans are terrestrial, but most live throughout Earth's oceans and estuaries. Around seventy species comprising the family Aeglidae live only in freshwater in several South American countries. The only other known freshwater anomuran is the hermit crab *Clibanarius fonticola*, found solely on the island of Espiritu Santo, Vanuatu, and first described in 1990.[2]

A carcinized anomuran, the Alaskan king crab (*Paralithodes camtschaticus*) at the Birch Aquarium, Scripps Institution of Oceanography, University of California, San Diego.

Ecuadorian hermit crab (*C. compressus*), preserved specimen.

The many species of Brachyura and Anomura have more in common than their ten legs and stalked eyes. Their reproductive systems and life cycles are also roughly similar, though not *too* similar, of course. Some species show high degrees of sexual dimorphism, with marked difference in colour, overall size or claw size; in others, the most obvious difference is the narrowness of the male abdomen, compared to the wider abdomen of the female. Some attract mates by emitting enticing pheromones; in other species, males court females by displaying their strength or prowess in waving their claws or burrowing effectively. Some mate once annually, some once in a lifetime, and those in tropical or deep-sea locales, without widely variable seasons, may be fertile year-round.

Mating usually takes place abdomen to abdomen, with the male clasping the female. Females receive sperm, which they can store for quite some time, in a packet known as a spermatophore.

Appendages on the males' first thoracic segment double as swimmerets, also known as pleopods, and as gonopods that deposit sperm into females' gonopores, the genital openings on her sixth thoracic segment. When the female is ready, her eggs proceed from the ovaries through oviducts, where they come into contact with stored sperm before being released. She holds the fertilized eggs on her abdomen in a cluster known as a sponge or berries. Most hermit crabs have to leave their shells – at least temporarily – to mate, and lay eggs that must be fertilized externally. The number of eggs laid varies by species but can number well into the thousands.

While males of some species guard females before or after mating, neither parent plays a parental role after the eggs mature. A mother crab's duties typically end when her babies hatch, though for the many species that live in intertidal zones or on land, she does go to some effort to make sure that they mature where they can easily ride a high tide out to sea. (An exception that proves the rule is *Metopaulias depressus*, a Jamaican crab that lives only in the water stored in the cup formed by the leaves of a bromeliad. Female crabs of this species lay relatively few eggs but take intensive care of their young.[3]) Taking their place among the zooplankton in open oceans, crab larvae can swim on their own and have developed eyes but make easy meals for other animals. At this stage, which can last as little as a month or as long as two years, depending on the species, larvae moult frequently. In the last larval stage, they become quite crab-like creatures, known as megalopa among the brachyurans, and glaucothoe if anomuran.

With the next moult, crabs take their adult forms. Brachyurans finally tuck their abdomens under their carapaces and the hermit crab finds his first mollusc shell. Intertidal and terrestrial crabs return to estuaries, mangrove forests and marshes like those where they hatched. They continue to grow by moulting, though

New crab larvum.

less frequently as they age. For each moult, the crab absorbs much of the shell's calcium into her soft tissues, weakening the shell, which eventually splits. The crab slips out of her old shell and rests, vulnerable to predators, while a new one forms. A Maryland blue crab might live only two to three years, even if it manages to avoid predators, including humans fishing for crab. A hermit crab can live for thirty years in the wild, but those captured by the pet trade have much shorter lifespans. A Japanese spider crab, the largest of all crabs, can live a century.

Other arthropods that we commonly refer to as crabs are not crustaceans at all. Horseshoe crabs do belong to the phylum Arthropoda (now often given as Euarthropoda), which includes a huge number of invertebrates that share features such as jointed legs and chitinous exoskeletons. Subphyla include Crustacea (shrimp, lobsters, crabs, barnacles and copepods, among others); Hexapoda (six-legged insects and springtails); Myriapoda (centipedes, millipedes and the like); Trilobitomorpha (the extinct trilobites); and Chelicerata (which includes scorpions, spiders, ticks, mites and horseshoe crabs). Members of these species are known as chelicerates, in recognition of their claw- or pincer-like mouthparts. Some chelicerates are venomous, and all lack antennae common to insects and crustaceans. Superficial morphological characteristics of this group vary tremendously. To a casual observer, spindly, long-legged spiders could seem to have little in common with the hefty horseshoe crab (family Limulidae), which

Atlantic horseshoe crab (*Limulus polyphemus*), Cape Cod, Massachusetts.

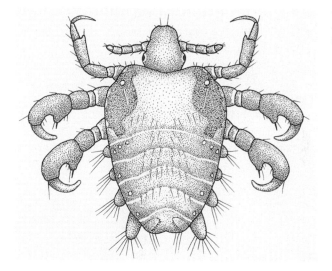

from afar resembles a brown soldier's helmet discarded on the beach or floating just offshore. Up close (and especially with a peek at its underside), the horseshoe crab's segmented body, jointed legs and hard shell might appear reminiscent of a crab to an observer at a loss to compare the creature to any other, despite a long caudal spine – a kind of tail that the horseshoe crab uses as a rudder – absent in true crabs. While there are thousands of species of true crabs and anomurans, there are only four extant horseshoe crabs, one of which occupies much of the Atlantic coast of North America and the Gulf of Mexico. The other three are found in South and East Asia, in waters from Japan to Indonesia to India.

At least one more creature is commonly called a crab, at least in the English language, although it is actually a six-legged insect. Pubic lice (*Pthirus pubis*), which cause intense itching when they infest the hair of human genital areas, are often referred to as crab

17

Trilobite fossil (*Chasmops odini*) collected from mid-Ordovician limestone, Osmussaar Island, Estonia.

1 cm

lice – or just 'crabs'. Most humans are probably appalled to find crab lice on their bodies. But not the narrator of Jean Genet's *Funeral Rites* (1948). Mourning the death of his young lover, he relishes the presence of these crabs as a reminder of their intimacy: 'It pleased me to think that they retained a dim memory of that same place on Jean's body, whose blood they had sucked.'[4] Genet uses the word *morpion* in the original French, which can refer to a louse, a naughty child or a game of noughts and crosses (tic-tac-toe). In English translations, readers are treated to the colloquial 'crab'. But that colloquialism derives from misrecognition. While in this volume I take a broad approach, the crab louse is at a far enough remove that I'll let this short passage suffice for this misnomered animal. The remainder of this book will explore the brachyuran crabs, the anomurans and the horseshoe crabs – their histories, their animal lives, their uses in human society and their cultural valence. Their history begins with a query into their origins.

Over half a billion years ago, invertebrates, including the first arthropods, were still in their earliest forms. The first creatures now classified as arthropods are the trilobites, which flourished worldwide from at least 540–520 MYA (millions of years ago) to just over 250 MYA. Trilobites may not have made it through the mass extinction event that marked the end of the Permian period, but other arthropods survived. The fossil record of the horseshoe crab, for example, dates back as far as the Ordovician period, thanks to a flurry of recent discoveries. In 2008, researchers in Manitoba, Canada, described a new genus in the order Xiphosuridae, which includes the extant family Limulus and some extinct relatives. They named their new species *Lunataspis aurora* and dated the fossils to 445 MYA.[5] In 2012, another team of researchers identified a new horseshoe crab ancestor – almost as ancient (425 MYA) – in Herefordshire, United Kingdom.[6] And throughout the early 2000s, publications extolled the rich contents of the Fezouata Formation in Morocco, after the fossil collector Mohamed Ben Moula introduced Belgian scientist Peter Van Roy

A deceased horseshoe crab, elderly enough to stop moulting and collect slipper limpets and other molluscs on her carapace.

(then a graduate student) to his findings. These fossils included previously unknown horseshoe crabs and many other forms of marine life from circa 485 MYA.[7] These ancestral horseshoes differ in many significant ways from their living descendants (for one thing, they were relatively tiny creatures, measuring just a few millimetres or centimetres in length). But the fossil record suggests remarkable similarity between long-extinct species such as *Limulus darwini*, first described by Adrian Kin and Błażej Błażejowski in 2014 after discovery in a quarry in Poland, and the extant *Limulus polyphemus*, the Atlantic horseshoe crab.

In both scientific and popular literature, horseshoe crabs are sometimes referred to as 'living fossils' in recognition of the longevity of their key morphological characteristics, but there is good reason to reject the term as misleading. For one thing, it is oxymoronic: a fossil is by definition the petrified remains of a dead animal or an impression of its remains – anything but living. For another, it suggests that evolution proceeds towards an end goal, a settled form that once perfected goes unchanged, but this view glosses over real adaptations occurring over long time periods. Darwin's contemporary Thomas Huxley adopted the term 'persistent type' for living creatures that strongly resembled their fossil counterparts.[8] More recently, Kin and Błażejowski proposed the term 'stabilomorph', meaning 'stable in structure', as a replacement for 'living fossil'.[9] Horseshoe crabs are, after all, very contemporary animals, living and breathing, even if by most accounts they have changed little over a hundred million years or more, thanks to effective adaptations, not evolutionary stasis.

Anomuran fossils are relatively scant, given the composition of their body parts, the types of habitats they tend to occupy and the fact that other animals frequently consume their remains, but there is a growing fossil record and other data to draw on. Phylogenetic studies, using both morphological and molecular analysis, suggest that Anomura emerged from 'a crab-like ancestor' in the late Permian period, around 259 MYA, before either dinosaurs or mammals walked the Earth.[10] At that time, Anomura diverged from Brachyura. Perhaps the oldest anomuran fossil collected to date is from an upper Triassic deposit (237–201.3 MYA) on the Musandam Peninsula that juts into the Persian Gulf, to the west, and the Gulf of Oman, to the east, at the northeast tip of the United Arab Emirates. The new species was named *Plattykotta akaina*. The find significantly prefigured the lower Jurassic specimen *Eocarcinus praecursor* collected in the twentieth century and once considered the oldest anomuran fossil.[11] Described by Thomas Henry Withers in 1932, the *E. praecursor* fossils were found in early Jurassic deposits in the north and southwest of England. Withers identified his discovery as brachyuran, but twenty-first-century scientists have generally regarded *E. praecursor* as ambiguous, more likely anomuran or possibly macuran (the group including lobsters and crayfish), based on characteristics including claws on the second as well as the first pereipods and articulating rings suggesting an abdomen that could not be tucked under the carapace.[12]

Anomurans radiated into several distinct groups in the late Triassic, with major groups of squat lobsters and hermit crabs developing, possibly filling the ecological niches vacated by trilobites that did not survive the mass extinction that ended the Permian period circa 252 MYA. They continued to diversify throughout the Jurassic, as new families of squat lobsters and porcelain crabs evolved. At least three separate times within Anomura, less crab-like creatures have evolved into quite crab-like animals ('carcinization', or what Lancelot Alexander Borradaile, the influential British zoologist active in the late nineteenth and early twentieth centuries, called 'the many attempts of nature to evolve a crab'[13]). For example, the family Porcellanidae apparently began to carcinicize from a squat lobster ancestor around 172 MYA, becoming more crab-like over the next 20 or 30 million years.

The oldest brachyuran fossils date to the early Jurassic period, roughly around the time that the supercontinent Gondwana broke up, although researchers tend to agree that Brachyura, like Anomura, has been around much longer, with origins in the Permian or Triassic. Murky origins result, in part, from the same conditions that limit the plentifulness of anomuran fossils. Moulted shells, comprised of chitin, and soft body parts are often consumed by other animals or by the moulted crab herself, or disintegrate rather than fossilize. Besides, crab habitats may not be conducive to forming fossils, nor to collecting them. But it is well established that by the middle Jurassic, Brachyura was well enough established to radiate into several distinct families and superfamilies, setting the stage for an 'evolutionary explosion' in the Late Jurassic.[14]

The oldest known brachyuran fossil, which hails from circa 190.8–182.7 MYA, is a single specimen of *Eoprosopon klugi* that was found in a clay pit in the northern part of the German state of Bavaria. First described by Reinhard Förster in 1986 and placed into the family Prosopidae, it was recategorized by Danièle Guinot as a member of Homolodromiidae. Almost three decades later, Joachim and Carolin Haug re-examined the *E. klugi* holotype using imaging techniques unavailable in the 1980s, which gave them a much more detailed glimpse of some aspects of the fossil. While confirming that some characteristics of the crab remain ambiguous, such as the structure of its eyes, they found enough qualities, such as the orientation of the moveable claw finger, and narrow abdominal sections (the pleomeres), to comfortably confirm *E. klugi*'s place in Brachyura.

Conventional wisdom regarding the evolutionary history of crabs is subject to constant revision as new evidence is, literally, dug up. Newly exposed fossils constantly challenge presumptions about when particular families emerged and relationships between families, and the number of known species, both extinct and extant, continues to grow. When in 2008 a team of scientists started visiting an abandoned quarry (once a coral reef) in the province of Navarre in northern Spain, they quickly identified 36 new species of decapods dating from the mid-Cretaceous, about 100 MYA. Two of their discoveries, named *Cretamaja granulata* and *Koskobilius postangustus*, provide the earliest known fossil evidence of the spider crab family Majoidea, displacing a specimen found in France previously known as the oldest spider crab.[15] Researchers were surprised by the age, abundance and diversity of signs of life in the old reef. Their findings suggest that the extent of what is known about such creatures only scratches the surface of what may someday be discovered.

Sometimes, where fossils are lacking, other traces of an animal's presence may be found. For example, biologists have studied crescent-shaped pits found in corals from Pilocenic and Pleistocenic formations in Cuba and the state of Florida. Lots of animals can make holes in coral, but none other than members of the Cryptochiridae family (the so-called 'gall crabs') is known to dig pits in this shape, accommodating the body in the thickest part of the crescent and the claws at its points. (Less frequently, a crab nestles against the coral and a 'gall' forms around her; typically, only females live in pits, and males roam free.) If these pits are not proper crab fossils, they are the evocative abandoned ruins of what was once an individual crab's home.[16]

Elsewhere, new data emerges from fresh looks at already known specimens. In a 2012 publication, a team led by Javier Luque revised standing knowledge about the Raninoida clade (the frog crabs). It was previously thought that the earliest constituents of this family took a 'necrocarcinid' form, with a broad

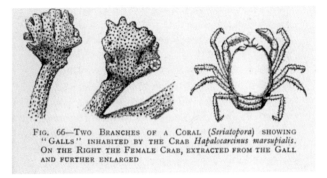

Fig. 66—Two Branches of a Coral (*Seriatopora*) showing "Galls" inhabited by the Crab *Hapalocarcinus marsupialis*. On the Right the Female Crab, extracted from the Gall and further enlarged

thoracic sternum and the pleon (abdomen) fully between the legs. In that view, it was only towards the end of the Lower Cretaceous period – specifically the Albian age (112–99.6 MYA) – that the 'fusiform' carapace now found in some species evolved, in an instance of decarcination; that is, the evolution of a crab towards a less conventionally crab-like form. (A fusiform body is elongated and narrower at its ends than its middle.) During the Albian, both necrocarcinid and fusiform frog crabs diversified and flourished, but necrocarcinid crabs weren't alone prior to the Albian age. Luque and other researchers dated fusiform crab fossils from the Paja Formation, which runs through the department of Santander in north-central Colombia, to the Aptian age (*c.* 115 MYA). Elsewhere, Luque has argued that some frog crabs may have evolved into fusiform types as they specialized in burrowing into benthic sediment as early as 125 MYA. This way of life may have helped frog crabs survive the mid-Aptian extinction event, which was marked by low-oxygen oceanic conditions, to which frog crabs are fairly tolerant.[17]

In another instance of crab history being rewritten because of the re-evaluation of a specimen, palaeontologist Greg Dietl of Cornell University happened by chance to notice fossils on display in a museum in Chiapas, Mexico, dated circa 67–69 MYA.[18] The specimen is unusually large for the Late Cretaceous, and its right claw much larger than the left. The dactyl, or moveable top 'finger' of the right chelae, is the 'crusher', or more powerful claw, and it has a tooth that some crabs use to open snail shells. The smaller left claw is of a dexterous type called a 'cutter', used to catch prey. The size of the animal, the asymmetry of its claws and the claw tooth were thought to have been Cenozoic adaptations that came some 20 million years later. Dietl's discovery pushed back the evolutionary clock, challenging earlier theories. His recognition that dimorphic claws and dactyl teeth evolved much earlier than previously thought reminds us just how little is known about the origins of crabs and other animals.

As if to prove just how great are the gaps in our knowledge of the history of crabs, in 2005 a team led by Javier Luque made a discovery so remarkable that it briefly became a minor Internet sensation. They dubbed their find *Callichimaera perplexa*, based on fossils found in both Colombia and the state of Wyoming dating to the mid-Cretaceous, around 95 to 90 MYA, that don't fit into any previously known group. Among other unusual characteristics, the chimera crab had huge, unprotected eyes, rather than a burrower's typically smaller and easily retractable eyes. Artists' renderings of what it might have looked like were so appealing – out-Disneying Disney, really – that this crab made a big splash in mainstream media outlets, taking up the mantle of the 'platypus of crabs'.[19]

As I watched news reports of the discovery of *C. perplexa* turn up everywhere from the *Daily Mail* to the *Washington Post* and countless science and nature blogs, all endlessly reposted on social media, I was delighted that I wasn't the only one – at least, not the only non-carcinologist – currently considering crab

Charlotte Seid, *White-spotted Hermit Crab (Dardanus megistos)*, 2017, watercolour and ink on paper.

history and following crab news. And yet the more I read, the more I realized how much I had yet to learn, and how many questions about the animals we call crabs remain unanswered, not only by a curious outsider like myself, but by leading experts in the field.

But answers to some of my questions were coming into focus. I began this chapter with a pair of questions about the hermit crabs I encountered in large numbers on a beach in Costa Rica. Where did they get their shells, I wondered? I didn't see a lot of empty shells on the beach, and I never witnessed one of these creatures trade in its shell for a larger mobile home, but it was easy enough to discover that the hermits have their own systems for taking care of the business of obtaining shells.

I also asked, is the hermit crab a crab? Exploring this question, I encountered systems of classification under constant revision and a scientific discipline (like any other scholarly endeavour, I suppose) in competitive and sometimes contentious pursuit of knowledge and ways of organizing it. I found groups of animals that were contemporaries of – and outlived – the dinosaurs (and in the case of horseshoe crabs, animals that long preceded the dinosaurs, too). I discovered families whose ancestors inhabited Pangea, Laurasia and Gondwana, and radiated globally as these supercontinents broke apart and drifted into the relative positions they have occupied from the early Cenozoic (starting 66 MYA) to the Anthropocene. These creatures sent me on a journey across aeons that I had barely previously imagined. And I learned of species too numerous to catalogue in this book. In the chapters that follow, I will share what I have learned about their lives and about how our human lives are entangled, in many places, with them.

2 Classifying Crabs

What pattern connects the crab to the lobster
and the orchid to the primrose and all the four
of them to me? And me to you?
Gregory Bateson, *Mind and Nature: A Necessary Unity* (1979)

In 1886, a young woman went to work at the Smithsonian Institution in Washington, DC, as a clerk. The job title hardly reflected the duties that Mary Jane Rathbun, 24, formerly of Buffalo, New York, quickly assumed. Mary had developed a taste for research when she started visiting Woods Hole, Massachusetts, with her brother Richard in 1881, where he worked with the U.S. Department of Commerce's Fish Commission (Woods Hole is now home to the acclaimed Marine Biological Laboratory, one of several key institutions in the marine sciences). Richard Rathbun also held the title of Curator of Marine Invertebrates at the Smithsonian. Eventually he became Assistant Secretary and then Secretary of the National Museum. Mary catalogued a rapidly growing collection and was promoted to Second Assistant Curator in 1898 and Assistant Curator in 1907. But she didn't just manage the office while others – mostly male scientists and explorers, including her brother – took off on far-flung expeditions to collect specimens that would come back to the museum. She dove headlong into crustacean taxonomy, eventually identifying 1,147 new crab species and 63 new genera.

Rathbun's achievement was nothing short of astounding. Compare, for example, the influential French carcinologist Danièle Guinot, who started her career in 1955 at the Muséum national d'Histoire naturelle in Paris, where she remains Professor Emeritus.

While Guinot conducted research on crab evolution, reproduction and behaviour, her primary contributions, like Rathbun's, are in taxonomy.[1] Over the course of her career, she named 164 new species, 61 new genera and twenty new supergenera. Patsy (Pat) A. McLaughlin (1932–2011), who ranked among the world's leading experts on hermit crabs, named 163 species, 37 genera and one family, and that's only counting her descriptions of new paguroids.[2] Both Guinot and McLaughlin's achievements add up to remarkable figures for anybody – but Rathbun.

Mary Jane Rathbun with crab, in 1937.

Still, species accounted for by these prolific researchers represent a fraction of known crab species. Even Aristotle, writing almost 24 centuries ago, recognized that they belong to large families: 'Of the crab, the varieties are indefinite and incalculable.'[3] A 1977 volume claimed that there were some 4,500 species of true crabs; just over two decades later, sources set the number much higher: 6,793 species of Brachyura and some 2,500 Anomura.[4] These numbers continue to grow. Likewise, their family tree continues to be subject to revision. There is no debate that crabs (of all types) belong to the phylum Arthropoda, which emerged

Blue crab fossil (genus *Callinectes* Rathbun), *c.* 1896.

over 500 MYA, when many of the continents still huddled together to form the supercontinent Gondwana. But the origins of and relationships among the creatures that we would come to know as crabs (Brachyura and Anomura, anyway) are far from settled. In her 1982 introduction to the landmark ten-volume treatise *The Biology of Crustacea*, Dorothy E. Bliss noted that crustacean systematics is marked by such intense 'ferment in the field' that any listing of families and their members is necessarily 'a compromise'.[5] The marine scientist and environmentalist Joel Walker Hedgpeth went so far as to quip that 'there is something about writing on arthropod phylogeny that brings out the worst in people.'[6] (It's tempting to ask, did he mean *crabbiness*?) But for some, the subject is a lifelong passion, marked by generosity and wonder.

In intervening decades, little seems to have changed. Systems of classification are by no means stable; they are, in many ways, claims, arguments, maps that shift and grow whenever new data confounds old categories. The advent of DNA testing has surely shed light on crab phylogeny, giving scientists new tools with which to examine relationships among – and differences between – closely related creatures. But a great deal of work in this area has been done through old-fashioned morphology – the study of the components and structure of organisms – now augmented by modern imaging technologies that bring out subtle details of fossil fragments.

The scientists who do this work are engaging in practices of getting to know non-human animals, their physiognomy, their relationships to one another, their histories – past and present. But given that they sometimes kill live animals to preserve as study specimens, not all of us may be entirely comfortable with their methods. My conversations with scientists working in these areas suggested that their relationships to the animals they study

Albrecht Dürer, *Crab*, 1495, gouache and watercolour on paper.

– in the form of live populations, as well as preserved specimens and fossils – are deeply thoughtful and long-lasting; intimate, really. They are all clearly motivated to understand Earth's biodiversity so that we might better protect it: that is, so that these animals have a future. I saw a great deal of 'ferment in the field' but little evidence that this kind of work necessarily 'brings out the worst in people', beyond the kinds of competition endemic to all professions. And I saw plenty to celebrate in terms of human achievements, in creating new knowledge in natural history and biodiversity science. Imagine how few of us will have the privilege of naming a new animal or plant, and how few of us have cross-species relationships lasting decades with non-human creatures other than domestic animals or livestock. How do these scientists know what they know about these animals? How does one dare declare a specimen previously unknown? I begin to explore this question and others in a brush with Mary J. Rathbun, and continue with a look at recently identified new species.

Visiting Washington, I sought to follow in Mary Rathbun's footsteps – for a few days, anyway. Like her, most of my time at the Smithsonian was spent at a desk, poring over paperwork or peering at preserved specimens. And like her, I started at the red brick building known as 'the castle', now a visitor's centre for a sprawling group of museums. It was hard to imagine the diminutive Rathbun huddled alongside other researchers and their specimens in this single building in the early years of her career: the Museum of Natural History didn't open until 1910, a project spearheaded by her brother Richard. The museum's collections eventually outgrew that imposing Neoclassical building too, and many of its research labs and specimens both wet (those preserved in alcohol solutions in jars) and dry (such as bones and surplus taxidermy) were relocated to facilities in a Maryland suburb of Washington long after Rathbun's retirement.

A treasure trove of an archive suggested what Rathbun's workaday life contained: receiving and analysing specimens; distributing copies of new publications to colleagues at museums and universities all over the world and receiving theirs in kind; corresponding with other carcinologists and debating with them the proper categorization of various specimens. And she wrote and submitted papers to scientific journals, the first in 1891, co-authored with James L. Benedict, then a senior member of the Marine Invertebrate staff, although it was likely 'largely the result of Miss Rathbun's labors'.[7] The paper, on the mud crab genus Paneopus, describes more than three dozen species, six of them new, and proposes lumping them into one genus rather than splitting them into two, as prominent carcinologist A. Milne Edwards had previously done.

Rathbun is said to have been the first woman to hold a post as full-time curator at the museum, a feat she accomplished with only a high school degree (although she was later awarded an honorary doctorate by Georgetown University). But she did have female peers in a typically male-dominated science. To mention just a few: isopod systematicist Harriet Richardson's career at the Smithsonian, which began in 1901, overlapped with Rathbun's. Katherine J. Bush, whose career in invertebrate science began in 1879 in Addison Emery Verrill's lab at the U.S. Fish Commission in Woods Hole, later earned a doctorate in zoology, the first awarded to a woman at Harvard, where she continued to work at the Peabody Museum. (Maybe zoological interests run in families; just as Mary Rathbun and her brother Richard both made their marks at the Smithsonian, Bush's sisters Lucy and Charlotte, and her brother-in-law Wesley Roswell Coe, all worked at the Peabody for a time.) Isabella Gordon, the 'Grand Old Lady of Carcinology', was the first woman named to a full-time research position at the Natural History Museum in London. She published prolifically and famously met Emperor Hirohito, himself an avid amateur marine biologist, during a visit to Japan in 1961.[8] Gordon met Rathbun, too, during a trip to the United States in 1927.

Waldo LaSalle Schmitt and Mary Jane Rathbun, c. 1920s.

Officially, Rathbun held her post at the Smithsonian only until 1914, when she resigned to free up her own salary so that the museum would hire Waldo Schmitt as an assistant in her division. She lived off a modest inheritance and continued to report to work almost until her death in 1943, except when she volunteered for the Red Cross during the First World War. Schmitt rose to the rank of Curator of the

Division of Marine Invertebrates by 1923, and eventually all of Zoology, working alongside Rathbun in Washington and – unlike his mentor – participating in expeditions to Alaska, Antarctica, the Galápagos Islands, South America and the Belgian Congo.

Usually Rathbun worked from specimens at the museum, but she went to Europe in 1896 to photograph specimens in other collections. In 1904, she went to Paris to complete a major monograph cataloguing freshwater crabs held by the Muséum national d'Histoire naturelle. Some of the Paris museum's specimens had been shipped to Washington; others were too delicate to make the trip.[9] Rathbun worked to map the crab's family tree, even after she stopped receiving a salary. In 1918, she completed the first of her four book-length publications, *The Grapsoid Crabs of America*, followed by volumes on spider crabs (1925), cancroid crabs (1930) and the 'Oxystomatous and allied crabs' (1937).[10] Each of these is a thick volume comprising hundreds of descriptions, illustrations and photographic plates that became indispensable for carcinologists around the world, noted for their meticulousness.

Meanwhile, Rathbun wrote dozens of scientific articles, working with specimens that came to the museum in great quantity and from many different sources. 'In a collection of Costa Rican crabs recently sent to the United States National Museum by Prof. Manuel Valerio of San Jose', she wrote, 'there is a *Pinnixa* different from any previously obtained . . . *Pinnixa valerii*, new species'.[11] 'From time to time', Rathbun noted in another publication, 'Dr Hubert G. Schenck of Stanford University has given to the National Museum various crustaceans from the Tertiary of Oregon.' Sorting through Schenck's batch of frog crab fossils, she identified four new species, one of which she named in honour of the donor, *Eumorphocorystes schencki*.[12] One of Rathbun's final publications described two new species, *Potamon (Geothatphusa) harvardi* and

P. (G.) amalerensis, in a report on specimens collected in Uganda and Kenya, two of the many nations she never visited herself even as she played a major role in organizing scientific knowledge about their aquatic lives.[13]

The archive tells a wonderful story about the massive body of knowledge produced by Rathbun. But, as with all archives, it also tells stories of dead ends, missed opportunities and unfinished business. In October 1926, Dr Carlotta J. Maury wrote to Rathbun from the Department of Geology at Cornell University, asking her to identify a crab found among samples taken from a site being explored for oil. Maury, consulting for Royal Dutch Shell, identified molluscs herself but sought Rathbun's help with crabs, and saw that she was paid for her time:

> I have a very interesting little crab from the Tertiary of Venezuela . . . I would very, very much like to have your opinion upon them. May I send them to you? . . . The Company is good for $10 a day so you could have a box of candy, as well as the intellectual interest. Besides you will like the little crab. It looks absurdly like a miniature bull dog.[14]

Two weeks later Rathbun replied, albeit with fewer flourishes, identifying one fossil as *Callinectes reticulatus* and guessing at the genera to which the others belonged.[15] The two women wrote back and forth several times regarding the age of the fossils. When Rathbun sent the fossils back, she admitted that she was 'dismayed' that Maury could not keep them for further study.[16]

In the summer of 1927, Maury sent Rathbun more fossils. In September, when Rathbun returned from her summer holiday, she identified them and told Maury that the museum wanted to have these specimens if possible, and that she would like to write

Fossil holotype *Zanthopsis rathbunae*, named by Carlotta Maury in honour of Mary Jane Rathbun.

up descriptions of the new species among them for publication. Maury replied in longhand, expressing regret and underlining in red: 'It is against the present interests of the Royal Dutch Shell Co. to have this information published, because of rival companies in the same field.' She regretfully asked Rathbun to return the fossils while keeping any information gleaned from them 'confidential'.[17]

Still, Maury continued to send Rathbun fossils. In 1931, Rathbun asked if she could write descriptions of the new species found in a batch of specimens 'against the day when any restrictions as to publication may be removed by the owners of the material'.[18] Clearly she was loathe to let new knowledge go unrecorded. Maury could only reply 'The Co. is *adamant* about not publishing . . . Such beautiful specimens! But I can only waft them a farewell kiss.'[19] At this point, their correspondence – or, at least the archived record of it – drops off. Then, five years later, Rathbun checked back with Maury, hoping for permission to include the new species found in the Royal Dutch Shell specimens in a 'report on certain Venezuelan fossil crustacea' that she was working on.[20] Maury, apologetic as ever, advised Rathbun to 'forget them'.[21] I doubt she ever did.

Mary Rathbun may have been much appreciated by colleagues near and far, but let's face it, the animals that she chose to study aren't exactly the charismatic megafauna – the lions and elephants, pandas and penguins, whales and sharks – that are the symbolic faces of conservation groups, the stars of nature films and TV shows. In 1928, in a letter to Hubert Lyman Clark, a curator at Harvard's Museum of Comparative Zoology, Rathbun congratulates him on giving invertebrates 'so much recognition . . . for here there is no space to spare for the exhibit of such lowly creatures'.[22] Sometimes the Smithsonian seemed too small for the less glamorous members of the animal kingdom. Years earlier, in 1911, illustrator Violet Dandridge had joined Rathbun on a summer holiday in Maine, with the trip resulting in a set of drawings to be exhibited at the Smithsonian. That was the plan,

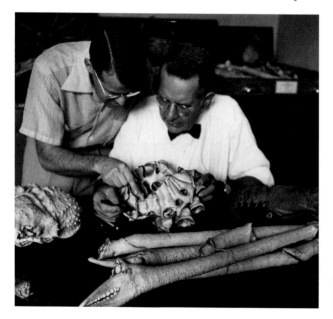

Waldo LaSalle Schmitt examining a giant crab.

anyway, until someone at the museum decided to replace the drawing show with a display of whale skeletons. Half a century later, Rathbun's colleague Waldo LaSalle Schmitt recalled the incident, complaining in a letter to the editor of the volume *Notable American Women* that it was a 'splendid exhibit conceived and installed under Miss Rathbun's watchful eye', and lamenting that the agenda of 'the vertebrate end of this Museum' took precedent over invertebrate interests: 'I can still work up a peeve over that performance.'[23]

In this regard, nothing much has changed. The Hall of Ocean in the Smithsonian's Museum of Natural History is cacophonous and crowded. Arranged mostly thematically, with installations on biodiversity, seamounts and the open ocean, among others, there are wondrous crabs here and there. In the hydrothermal vent display, the long spikes of a preserved porcupine crab (*Neolithodes grimaldii*) press against the walls of its jar. Some tiny – and very much alive – red hermit crabs occupy the only aquarium in the hall. In a small diorama representing a Chesapeake Bay shore, replicas of juvenile and adult blue crabs hide and feed. There's no mention of Rathbun's significant intervention into the muddled science of the blue crab's family ties, in a paper that refutes several other names given to the species by authors confused by juvenile specimens, and lands once and for all on a name, *Callinectes sapidus*, which translates as 'beautiful, savoury swimmer', befitting of the popular Western Atlantic crab.[24]

Rathbun's 'lowly creatures' may be unlikely to wow crowds or draw in donors (compare the O. Orkin Insect Zoo, named in honour of Otto Orkin, founder of the pest control company, upon a $500,000 donation in 1992, or the David H. Koch Hall of Human Origins and the David H. Koch Hall of Fossils – Deep Time, which resulted from gifts of $15 and $35 million in 2009 and 2012, respectively, from the fossil fuel billionaire known for funding groups promoting climate change denial and for opposing federal environmental regulations.[25] It would be an understatement to say that David Koch and his brother Charles's political and economic agendas have been in many respects incompatible with the missions of museums devoted to scientific veracity and environmental justice.) Fortunately, dedicated scientists around the world continue to study crabs and other marine invertebrates, despite their sidekick status. Some of them are making new discoveries so unusual that they would amaze Rathbun and her peers, challenging the bounds of what is known about crabs and crab-like creatures.

New crabs continue to be named, year after year. Some are truly new discoveries – that is, extinct or living animals previously unknown to humans, located only when new sites, such as parts of the ocean floor or unexcavated fossil deposits, are explored. Many are familiar to people living in or near an animal's habitat, but have only recently been entered into the scientific record. Others have been previously described but are being newly distinguished

Blue crab (*Callinectes sapidus* Rathbun 1896) specimen collected in 1931, at the Smithsonian Institution's Museum Support Center.

Porcupine crab (*Neolithodes grimaldii*) on display at the National Museum of Natural History, Washington, DC.

from closely related species and thus renamed. It's no small feat to identify a new species. The process is time-consuming and requires vast knowledge of any given class of animals, as well as a bit of taxonomic chutzpah to make a claim of newness. At least one scientist told me that they had forgone opportunities to describe and name new species because doing so just didn't interest them as much as other types of research, or because the laborious process took too much time and resources away from work they considered more urgent. For others, identifying new species is a career highlight. Some of these scientists' recent publications have revealed aspects of crustacean life – and history – previously unimagined.

Just as there was, in the late nineteenth century as Rathbun's career was getting started, a boom in exploration – collecting and research that allowed for the identification of countless new species – a similar wave of discovery took place in the twenty-first century. Starting in 2000, thanks to seed money from the philanthropic Alfred P. Sloan Foundation, a network of nearly 3,000 scientists from over eighty nations participated in a decade-long Census of Marine Life, conducting hundreds of expeditions and identifying as many as 6,000 new species, most of which have yet to be described.

On one such expedition, researchers aboard the *Alvin*, a type of submarine known as a human-operated or deep-submergence vehicle, diving at a depth of some 2,000 m (6,562 ft) along the East Pacific Rise and Pacific Antarctic Ridge near Easter Island in 2005, observed and then collected a white crustacean with lengthy chelipeds and a carapace longer than it is broad. The animal they found is also notably setose, that is, having hair-like bristles, especially on its legs, so much so that they dubbed the animal *Kiwa hirsuta*, now commonly known as the 'yeti' crab. Researchers identified this abominable snowman of the deep as

Costa Rican yeti crab (*Kiwa puravida*) with juvenile, photographed in 2017 by Greg Rouse of the Scripps Institution of Oceanography, collected by Erik Cordes during a dive in the Human Occupied Vehicle *Alvin* aboard the research vessel *Atlantis,* operated by Woods Hole Oceanographic Institution.

an anomuran, a squat lobster to be more precise. They saw that *K. hirsuta*, like many crabs, seems to have an omnivorous appetite and is willing to scavenge, but also that its hairy arm-like claws collect nutritious bacteria that flourish around hydrothermal vents (an ocean-floor phenomenon known only since about 1977).[26] You might say they wear their snacks on their sleeves.

Just a year later, members of another expedition connected to the Census of Marine Life were aboard the same sub, the *Alvin*, off the coast of Costa Rica, when they found another yeti-like crab 1,000 m (3,281 ft) below the surface. Andrew Thurber and his team named the new crab *Kiwa puravida*, from a Costa Rican saying meaning 'pure life'. *K. puravida* is similar in many ways to *K. hirsuta* but has a more prominent tooth on its rostrum and a distinctly larger and more cleft telson (the rear-most segment of its abdomen), among other distinguishing characteristics. If the

Costa Rican yeti crabs in natural habitat, photographed in 2019 by Greg Rouse of SIO and the Schmidt Ocean Institute from the remotely operated vehicle *SuBastien* aboard the R/V *Falkor*, operated by the Schmidt Institute of Oceanography. With chemosynthetic mussels, deep-sea shrimp, king crabs and tube worms.

team that discovered the first yeti crabs recognized that they might eat bacteria that collect on their bristled claws, Thurber's team went a step further, reporting that *K. puravida* doesn't forage (at least, not much) but actually *farms* the bacteria, waving its claws around methane seeps, effectively encouraging the growth of the desired bacteria and making it easier to harvest.[27]

In 2010, a third team of researchers came across yet another yeti crab around hydrothermal vents at a depth of 2,600 m (8,530 ft) at the East Scotia Ridge, between the Southern Ocean and Antarctica. *Kiwa tyleri* (named after the University of Southampton scientist Paul Tyler, who specialized in deep-sea subjects) is stoutly rounded, in comparison to its relatively elegant and elongated cousins, with blocky claws and short, dense fuzz instead of long furry bristles. They use this fuzz – their own uniquely adapted form of setae – to farm and harvest bacteria, but they differ in many ways from their *Kiwa* kin, in behaviour as well as in appearance. *K. hirsuta* and *puravida* give members of their own species some personal space, but *K. tyleri* pack together in swarms around vents in communities of hundreds or even thousands of individuals, forming white, ghostly clumps of churning life on the ocean floor.[28]

The Census of Marine Life coordinated funding and informational support for exploration of the Earth's oceans, which cover over 70 per cent of the planet's surface, the majority of which is unmapped. Humans really know very little about that part of our world and the creatures that live there. But life on our landmasses also poses many mysteries, and researchers have come across many of the species that live with us on land only recently. For example, *Kani maranjandun*, an arboreal crab that lives in flooded tree hollows in the mountain range known as the Western Ghats in India, was first described in 2017. Members of the Kani (or Kanikkaran) tribes that live in the Agasthyavanam Biological Park have long been familiar with these extraordinary creatures and use small numbers of them to make oils with medicinal properties. They helped a research team conducting a survey of Ghat forests to locate these crabs and collect specimens, and the genus was named in their honour. *K. maranjandun* – the species name

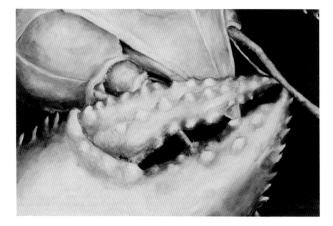

Lily Simonson,
Kiwa puravida,
2012, oil on canvas.

43

comes from the words for 'tree' and 'crab' in Malayalam, the language of the Indian state of Kerala – is a handsome crab, blue-black on the dorsal side and yellow-orange underneath, with very long walking (should we say climbing?) legs whose terminal dactyl sections have little hooks, like an arborist's spurs. Most so-called tree crabs hang out in holes in tree trunks or on shrubbery close to the ground but do most of their foraging for food on the ground and visit nearby streams for fresh water. 'True' arboreal crabs, ones that spend their entire life cycle in trees, are far more rare. *K. maranjandun* has been seen 10 m (33 ft) high in trees, and juveniles even shelter in tree canopies. Researchers were hardly surprised to find a previously undescribed creature in the forests of the Western Ghats, a relatively little-studied biodiversity 'hotspot' recognized as containing a high concentration of diverse plant and animal life that is, in places, extremely vulnerable. There are almost certainly many other species – including crabs, no doubt – known only to indigenous locals, or perhaps to no humans at all.[29]

The three new species of yeti crab forming the genus *Kiwa* opened up a whole new branch of crustacean life and, given that

The arboreal crab *Kani maranjandun* of the Western Ghats, India.

44

they live at the ocean floor, it's quite likely that the researchers who authored the first published descriptions of these animals, and their colleagues on the expeditions that first encountered them, were the very first humans to observe them. In contrast, the *Kani* tree crab was well known to indigenous peoples of the Western Ghats, who shared some of their knowledge of it with researchers affiliated with institutions in South and Southeast Asia, the University of Kerala and National University of Singapore. In both cases researchers encountered live animals and collected some of them to preserve as specimens to be placed in museum collections for future study. But a great many new species are found much the same way that Mary Rathbun did her work, comparing hundreds of specimens, preserved and in fossil forms, newly collected or archived in museums around the world.

Sometimes the work of sorting out what constitutes a new species or genus takes place gradually, over the course of many decades, in the hands of several generations of scientists. Most of us are familiar with hermit crabs that, instead of bearing a crusty exoskeleton, shelter within empty mollusc shells; after all, they are commonly sold as pets in the aquarium trade. (Whether having a hermit crab as a pet is a good idea or not is another question, and there are many reasons to think that the answer to that question should be no: since they don't breed in captivity, all hermit crabs sold as pets are culled from their natural habitats, and not all suppliers handle them ethically. They live naturally in large colonies, but most kept captive are alone or with only one or two other crabs. Many unskilled owners don't maintain proper levels of humidity, which contributes to severely shortened lifespans – in the wild they can live thirty years or more. Painted shells, popular among those new to hermit crabs, can be toxic to the animals.[30]) But not all hermit crabs appropriate the abandoned shells of dead animals as their homes. There are 'blanket crabs' that literally snuggle up with a symbiotic sea anemone. Another hermit crab, *Diogenes heteropsammicola*, found in Oshima Strait in southern Japan, takes a living coral rather than an uninhabited shell as its home.

The blanket-hermit long known as *Paguropsis typica* was first identified by J. R. Henderson, a Scottish biologist who held a post at the Christian College of Madras, India, where he wrote up his report on the animal, using a specimen found in the Philippines. Henderson had taken on the task of analysing a small set of anomuran specimens collected during the global voyage of the HMS *Challenger*, which from late 1872 to 1876 sailed the Earth's oceans with a scientific crew.[31] Independently, in 1899, Alfred William Alcock, then British Superintendent of the Imperial Museum (now the Indian Museum) at Kolkata, described a similar species from the seas off South India that he first thought to be unique, but by 1901 came to believe was identical to the one identified by Henderson. (Clearly, marine biology was one of countless endeavours in which resources and knowledge flowed through and to colonial institutions in this era.)

Over a century later, Rafael Lemaitre of the Museum of Natural History at the Smithsonian Institution helped to show that Alcock was right in the first place. His *Paguropsis andersoni* and Henderson's *P. typica* are distinct species. And they aren't alone in the unusual behaviour of covering their bodies with another living creature. Lemaitre, who grew up in a coastal region of Colombia, was always drawn to the ocean and pursued marine biology as an undergraduate, eventually relocating to the University of Miami where he studied under Pat McLaughlin, the prolific hermit crab expert. In the 1990s McLaughlin began to visit the Muséum national d'Histoire naturelle in Paris to see specimens recently collected in the South Pacific and Indian Oceans. One of the compelling discoveries among the Paris collections was a relative treasure trove of blanket-hermit crabs. Henderson and Alcock had worked with just a handful of specimens. Now hundreds of blanket-hermits were available – eventually, the team working on this project studied 1,042 specimens.[32] Unfortunately McLaughlin died in 2011, but Lemaitre and others continued to study these unusual animals.

Anderson's 'blanket crab' (*Chlaenopagurus andersoni*), illustrated in Alfred W. Alcock, *Naturalist in Indian Seas* (1902).

The variations observed among these specimens, and others obtained for comparison from other museums, showed that Henderson was right the first time: *P. andersoni* deserved to be 'resurrected' as its own species. Not only that, but Lemaitre and others were able to identify five entirely new species. Some of the newly named animals were placed in a new genus, too: *Paguropsina pistillata* and *P. inermis*; the others, *Paguropsis gigas*, *P. lacinia* and *P. confusa*, were said to belong in the same genus as the *P. typica* and *P. andersoni*. Unlike many scientists who prefer to name newly described animals after other scientists, mentors or even the occasional celebrity, Lemaitre chose descriptive names evoking these crabs' characteristics: *pistillata* is the smallest species of the bunch; *inermis* is 'unarmed', indicating that its fourth pereopod is smooth, lacking the cutting-edge spines of its cousins; *gigas* is the largest of the bunch, growing up to 23 mm (0.9 in.) in length; *lacinia* refers to fringed setae found on one limb. And *P. confusa*? Lemaitre says this was the species 'most difficult to tease out', given its similarities to, especially, *P. andersoni*.[33]

Blanket-hermits are curious creatures. They are tiny, to begin with. For example, Lemaitre's *P. typicus* specimens ranged from 3.6 to 14.6 mm (0.14 to 0.57 in.) in length, measured across the shield (or carapace). They are more symmetrical than hermit crabs who have to coil their abdomens into snail shells, and like the character Linus van Pelt in Charles Schulz's *Peanuts* cartoons, they never go anywhere without their blankets. Unusual, to be sure, but they are far from the only animal, or even the only genus

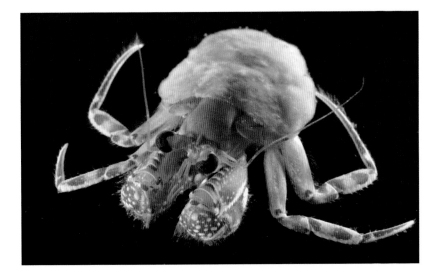

A blanket-hermit crab (*Paguropsis confusa*).

of crab, to live in mutualistic symbiosis – as friends with practical benefits – with another animal. Decorator crabs, for example, maintain gardens of live plants and animals on their shells, and boxer or pom-pom crabs carry tiny anemones in their claws at all times. But using a live animal as a protective covering is a rare behaviour indeed. If it is commonly said that a shell-using hermit crab carries her home on her back, the blanket-hermit's anemone might be seen as more ready-to-wear clothing than rigid housing. ('Nature is weird,' Lemaitre told me, with obvious affection for these animals.) It takes special adaptations to pull off this feat, which the blanket-hermits have in the form of a pair of small fourth thoracic legs that have at their tips two fingers with sharp teeth, sometimes likened to a bear's claw, that allow them to grasp and manipulate their anemones, just as we humans might pull blankets over our heads or push them down below the shoulders.

Newly abundant specimens were a boon to Lemaitre and other blanket-hermit crab researchers, but they also had another tool that was not commonplace when Henderson and Alcock were working: colour photography. Specimens collected from the wild – a practice that generally requires permits from local conservation authorities – are frequently preserved immediately. The animal is sedated or exposed to chilly temperatures, which has a similar effect, then injected with a fixative such as formaldehyde to prevent rot. Finally, it is stored in an alcohol solution, usually in labelled, clear glass jars. In this process, crabs lose their colours. Wet preserved specimens can range from ghostly white to murky ochre, lacking the bright reds, yellows, blues, stripes, dots and other variations found in live animals. Likewise, the anemones that pair with blanket-hermits fade. But the new specimens that Lemaitre studied were photographed in all their resplendent colours before preservation, providing clues about differences between species unknowable to previous researchers. In fact,

Preserved crab specimens at the Smithsonian Institution's Museum Support Center, Suitland, Maryland.

being able to compare coloration is what led to the recognition that *P. andersoni* and *P. confusa* are different species: the former is bright enough, in shades of orange and with white edges, but the latter is even more brilliantly hued in oranges and pinks, variegating along the legs.

Lemaitre's work on blanket crabs mostly involved preserved specimens. But sometimes researchers make new discoveries about very old creatures, ones long extinct and available only in fossil form. When Javier Luque ran across some unusual fossils in central Colombia in 2005, he knew right away that he had something special – or especially weird – but he wasn't quite sure what it was. He only knew that it dated to the mid-Cretaceous period, circa 90–95 MYA, and that it didn't look like anything else he had ever seen. The find was astonishing, for several reasons. First, the mysterious fossils were unusually intact, virtually complete, providing researchers with detailed evidence of the form of these animals' sex organs, antennae, mouthparts and eyes. Luque was able to collect several dozen specimens over the next decade, some of which came from over 6,400 km (4,000 mi.) away, in western Wyoming.

While Luque grew confident that the animal was a crustacean, he had to admit that the animal didn't fit easily into any known groups. Its mouthparts are like those of a shrimp. It seems to share some superficial traits with *Raninidae*, but its paddle-like legs are more like those of sea scorpions or swimming crabs than those of the burrowing ranid frog crabs. Likewise, Luque's discovery has a body longer than it is wide, with a tail not typically found in adult crabs, but common in crab larvae – and lobsters. No wonder, when it came time to name the animal, Luque landed on *Callichimaera perplexa*, which means 'beautiful, perplexing chimera'. However perplexing, when it was described in a 2019 publication the authors claimed it as a true brachyuran occupying its own new

genus, family and superfamily. They accounted for some of its outlying characteristics as an instance of neoteny, meaning the retention of characteristics from larval stages. Alternatively, they left open the possibility that the chimera crab might actually occupy an infraorder of its own between Anomura and Brachyura, which they dubbed *Callichimaeridea*.[34] In other words, these tiny (4–10 mm, or 0.16–0.39 in. wide) creatures seem to constitute either an instance of decarcinization with unique adaptations – 'a unique offshoot' – or a kind of missing link between two closely related groups.

Fifteen years may seem like a long time to wait between finding such a novel new species and entering it into the scientific record through final publication of the description. But 'you can imagine', Luque told me, 'for a group like crabs with more than 10,000 species known and an astonishing diversity of forms, the enterprise was long, exhausting, and at times frustrating'. (So much so that Luque later referred to the crab as his 'beautiful nightmare'.[35]) Of course, the chimera crab wasn't the only object of Luque's interest all those years – he also conducted research and

Artist's rendering of *Callichimaera perplexa* by Oksana Vernygora.

Unidentified king crab (genus *Paralomis*), photographed by the laboratory of Greg Rouse of Scripps Institution of Oceanography and collected by Greg Rouse and Avery Hatch during a dive in the HOV *Alvin* aboard the R/V *Atlantis*, operated by the Woods Hole Oceanographic Institution, at a methane seep off the Pacific Coast of Costa Rica at 1,800 metres (5,900 ft) in 2018.

published extensively on other animals, while leading the exhaustive investigation of the *C. perplexa* fossils, and slowly introducing the new creature to fellow scientists when presenting at conferences or lecturing at universities. *C. perplexa*'s debut was worth the wait: it is both a category-shaking discovery that, in Luque's words, 'is forcing us to rethink what makes a crab a "crab"', and a pop-science star.[36] How often does a new publication in carcinology grab headlines that tout the discovery as 'the strangest crab that ever lived', 'utterly bizarre', 'rule-breaking' and 'a beautiful mess of an animal'?[37]

In the case of Maury's Venezuelan crab fossils, new knowledge didn't make it into the scientific literature or the public record, despite Rathbun's best efforts. Despite her unparalleled work in brachyuran taxonomy, those are the little old crabs that got away from her – and perhaps, if they haven't turned up again in another researcher's hands, from all of us. The stumbling block that thwarted her quest to describe the new species from Venezuela was a profit-seeking corporation's proprietary control of material artefacts: a form of censorship. That embargo on knowledge should be shocking.

But there are, of course, many reasons other than corporate greed or indifference why we humans don't recognize all of the other animals that we share this planet with. Some we've misidentified. Still, workers like Mary Rathbun, Pat McLaughlin, Danièle Guinot, Rafael Lemaitre, Javier Luque and many others devote their careers to exploring relationships among animals, lumping together and splitting, grouping and carefully distinguishing species. Scientists like those I've mentioned in this chapter are part explorers, part detectives of the diversity in the crab corner of the natural world. That diversity has been recognized since at least Aristotle's era, but scientists continue to produce new knowledge about it. And they appear to do so with fascination – or at least, with less crabbiness than Joel Walker Hedgpeth as he approached taxonomic debates. Why shouldn't research in this area be a source of intellectual glee? After all, we make up the pigeonholes of this genus or that, old species or new. We quibble over these distinctions with each other, not with the categorized creatures. Most unidentified species, though, we just haven't encountered yet. Some we never will.

THE NIGHTMARE.

3　Are Crabs Crabby?

> Now, storytellers and Chesapeake Bay blue crabs have
> something in common: they usually approach what they're
> after sideways.
> John Barth, 'Historical Fiction, Fictitious History, and Chesapeake Bay
> Blue Crabs, or, About Aboutness', *Washington Post*, 15 July 1979

The crab appears in myth and metaphor as a grumpy, single-minded and somewhat unpleasant figure. In astrology, those born under the sign of Cancer are said to be moody, broody homebodies. In popular culture, where the crab makes fewer appearances than some creatures we might find more cuddly and more familiar, the crab has some honourable personality traits – loyalty, foremost – but is equally irritating. If fictional crabs are anything like the species that they are based on, then real-life crabs are nervous, quarrelsome animals. Hence the common use of the term 'crabby' to describe someone who is ill tempered, an English-language adjective since the sixteenth century, preceded similarly by 'crabbed', dating from thirteenth-century Middle English. William Shakespeare drew on the correlation between bad temper and certain crustaceans in *The Two Gentlemen of Verona* (*c*. 1589–93), naming the character Launce's notoriously disloyal dog 'Crab'. His master laments: 'I think Crab, my dog, be the sourest-natured dog that lives.'

Humans are expert at projecting our desires and fears onto each other and onto other beings, and we have a long tradition of developing myth, fable, parable and more from our observations of animal behaviour. Maybe those stories reveal kernels of truth here and there. Maybe they are convenient, embellished tales that cast the crab in roles she wasn't really born to play. As

Illustration for
'The Nightmare'
by James Freyberg,
in *The Un-natural
History Not Taught
in Bored Schools*
(1883).

Maryland waterman Grant Corbin told William Warner, author of a classic book about blue crabs called *Beautiful Swimmers*, 'nobody knows nothing about crabs . . . Might think they do, but they don't.'[1] What is really happening in the mind of a crab? Can the creature be said to have a mind at all? Can we ever know?

In ancient Greek and Roman mythology, the crab is a fierce, devoted soldier, but ultimately vulnerable. In the second of the Twelve Labours of Heracles (or Hercules), Heracles faces the Lernaean Hydra, a multi-headed sea serpent raised by his stepmother and nemesis Hera. Angered that her stepson seems likely to defeat the monster, Hera sends the giant crab Karkinos (Latinized as Carcinus) to aid the hydra. The crab pinches the foot of Heracles, trying to distract him for long enough to give the hydra an advantage. But Heracles kills Karkinos with a blow, cracking his shell, and then slays the hydra. In some versions Heracles propels Karkinos into the sky with a powerful kick; in others Hera places the crab in the heavens in gratitude for his sacrifice – even if it was ultimately ineffectual. Accordingly, Cancer is moderate in size and the least luminous of the zodiacal constellations.

In another celestial myth, Poseidon charges Crios, an immortal giant crab, with the task of guarding his fifty daughters, the sea nymphs. When some of the nymphs steal past Crios, he seeks help from Vamari, the giant squid. Instead of bringing the missing nymphs home, the squid eats those he finds at sea. Crios, realizing he has been tricked, attacks Vamari. While the crab eventually prevails, he is badly wounded. Poseidon honours Crios' service by relieving him of pain and placing him safely among the stars. The spot he finds in the sky is a modest one, tucked between the much brighter constellations Leo and Gemini.

These mythic crabs are loyal, well-meaning and pugnacious. They are also a little bit bumbling – minor characters – and never stars of the show or the skies. Likewise, in astrology derived from

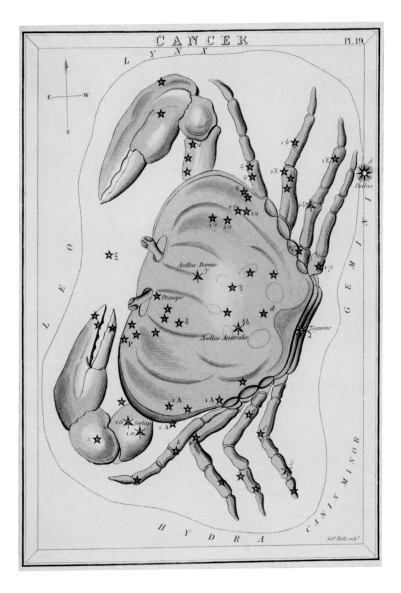

Sidney Hall sculp.t

Bronze crab, 3rd–1st century BCE, Greece. Possibly the base of a lamp.

Hellenic tradition, Cancerians (born from about 22 June to 22 July) are said to be, at their best, intuitive, insightful, nurturing and dependable. At their worst, those of us who were born under the sign of Cancer are overprotective, temperamental, sentimental and possessive. Jyotisha, the Vedic system of astrology, also recognizes the crab, Karka, but crustaceans are missing from the Chinese zodiac. At least one humourist insists that Cancer is 'objectively the worst star sign', having been saddled with 'the absolute trifecta of shit characteristics. The star sign shares its name with a terminal illness, it's visually represented as a crab or 69 or both, and its most readily identifiable characteristic is, like, weepiness', none of which look good in an online dating profile.[2] Like Karkinos and Crios, Cancerians are faithful to a fault, tough under pressure, but not quite the hero.

Speaking of the use of the term 'cancer' for any number of diseases that, broadly speaking, are caused by abnormal cell growth, historians date the use of that term to the Greek physician Hippocrates (c. 460–370 BCE). He used the terms *karkinos*

Sidney Hall, *Cancer*, from *Urania's Mirror; or, A View of the Heavens,* a series of astronomical star chart cards, 1824.

and *karkinoma* to describe tumours marked by swollen veins, which he likened to the many legs of a crab. At least, this is the version of the origins of the metaphorical name popularized in the medical writings of Galen of Pergamon (129–*c*. 200–216 CE). Or maybe Hippocrates found tumours hard like the crab's shell. These explanations draw inspiration from the crab's appearance, but there are also those who would liken the disease's pertinacity to the crab's legendary stubbornness.

In popular culture, crabs are just as tenacious as in ancient myth, often cast as supporting players and rendered so ambiguously that it is difficult to be convinced of their crabness. No crab appears in the original fairy tale *The Little Mermaid* (1837) by Hans Christian Andersen. Disney's animated adaptation, released in 1989, created a character named Sebastian the Crab, who doubles as an orchestra leader and as a sidekick to King Triton. Sebastian is charged with responsibility for looking out for the king's daughter, Ariel, just as Crios was meant to guard Poseidon's nymphs. Sebastian's musical influences are Jamaican reggae and Trinidadian calypso, but his crustacean roots are murkier. Lobster-like in some aspects (an elongated shell, a head separate from his thorax, and outsized symmetrical claws), Sebastian is further de-carcinized by the anthropomorphic features of his

Cuddly crab
plush toy.

face (googly eyes with white sclera and a tooth-baring grin). More convivial than most crab characters, he does retain some stereotypical traits: he is nervous and irritable.

Another pop-culture crab is just as ambivalently crab-like: Dr John Zoidberg, a character on *Futurama*, an animated series created by Matt Groening for Fox (1999–2003) and Comedy Central (2008–13), is a 'Decapodian', but if he has more than two walking legs and two clawed hands, they must be hidden under his lab coat. Incompetent, unlikeable, grossly omnivorous and offensively smelly, Zoidberg has referred to himself as a crab: in the episode 'Stench and Stenchability', upon cutting his own arm with his claw, he cries, 'Ouch, I forgot I was a giant crab' – but other episodes liken him to a lobster.

In Nickelodeon's animated television program *SpongeBob SquarePants* (1999–present), the unmistakably crab-like character Mr Krabs is the greedy owner of a fast food restaurant. He is prone to outbursts directed at his employees but is also a devoted parent to his daughter, who happens to be a sperm whale. The episode 'Kracked Krabs', in which Mr Krabs competes for an award from the League of Cheapskate Crabs, makes clear that miserliness is a trait of the species, not simply the individual. Bright red, like Sebastian, Mr Krabs appears to have only two walking legs (plus large claws, used as hands) when standing still, but in scenes where he walks, a motion blur effect and rapid clicking or chattering sound effects suggest the multiple legs of a crab. At least he has stalked eyes.

Occasionally crabs become, in our fantasies, actual villains. In the Australian Children's Television Foundation's 2002 superhero series *Legacy of the Silver Shadow*, the Crab is a former industrialist hell-bent on world domination, grooming his granddaughter Crab Girl to carry on his evildoing, but other than their red costumes, there isn't much crab to their characters. Just as

improbably, crabs embody our worst fears in Roger Corman's
low-budget monster movie *Attack of the Crab Monsters* (1957).
Grown to enormous proportions after exposure to radiation from
nuclear weapons testing like that actually conducted on Bikini
Atoll by the United States, Corman's fantastical crabs occupy a
small South Pacific island and feed on teams of scientists sent to
study the impact of radiation on the area. But they don't just get
nourishment from their prey; they eat their brains, absorb their
intelligence and develop the capacity to communicate telepath-
ically with humans. They want to destroy human life, but their
ceaseless burrowing threatens to destroy the island they live on;
their single-mindedness leads to their downfall.

The crabs I've mentioned aren't the only ones to appear in
popular culture. Among the best known is Jimmy, a blue crab in
James Michener's epic novel *Chesapeake* (1976). In Michener's
florid hands, Jimmy moults and mates in painstaking detail until
the 1886 flood that swelled the Susquehanna River dumps a 'vast

Another low-budget horror film featuring giant crabs: *Queen Crab* (dir. Brett Piper, 2015).

cesspool' of human and industrial waste into the Chesapeake Bay: Jimmy, his mate, and some of the people who eat their kin don't survive the toxins. (Could it be a coincidence that novelist John Barth, while claiming not yet to have read Michener's book, quipped that 'most historical fiction is a pretty fishy rendition of a crab', not long after its publication?[3]) You might find a crab or two in Lewis Carroll's *Alice's Adventures in Wonderland* (1865) or even in one of the video games based on it, such as the horror-adventure *Alice: Madness Returns* (2011), where you can encounter the cigar-chomping Cannon Crab. There are annoying little crabs in the Disney/Pixar film *Finding Nemo* (2003) that hang out on sewer pipes, pester passers-by and don't really want to help find Nemo. And there are sometimes crabs, in droves, in Disney's *Peter Pan* spin-off, the cartoon TV series *Jake and the Never Land Pirates* (2011–16). King Crab is the bearded, boastful leader of King Crab Island, not far from Never Land. 'I used to be the prince of pinch. Now . . . I'm the royal claw!', he sings, living up to expected stereotypes. It is perhaps only the same series' occasional appearances by Snappy the Hermit Crab that go against the grain: Snappy, who inhabits a pink shell with purple polka dots, is friendly and gentle. (In our imaginations, maybe it is only brachyurans that are crabby.)

There is, despite all these stories to the contrary, one myth in which crabs are honoured heroes who became wartime martyrs: it is said that Heike warriors who died at sea in the Battle of Dan-no-ura in 1185 are reincarnated as Heike-gani, the *Heike*

Crab Louie, the Prince of Crab Island, and his father King Crab in the 2015 'Crabageddon' episode of *Jake and the Never Land Pirates*.

(formerly *Dorippe*) *japonica*. No wonder. The dorsal carapace of the Heike or samurai crab has a set of ridges that happen to recall a grimacing face, outlining eyes, full cheeks and a round mouth. Obviously, the souls of the lost warriors found their way into these oceanic crabs.

Evolutionary biologist Julian Huxley, in an article in *Life* magazine in 1952, came up with another intriguing explanation for how the Heike came to carry faces on their backs. He suggested that Japanese fishermen, out of respect for the Heike warriors, had long thrown back crabs that most resembled the samurai, and taken only the less humanoid as food. Huxley's tale is a clever tale of artificial selection, in which humans control animal breeding, as for livestock or domestic animals. If it were true that crabs without samurai-faced shells were removed and therefore unable to reproduce as much as those with samurai-faced shells, then that trait would become more pronounced in future generations. Astronomer Carl Sagan picked up the story in his book *Cosmos* (1980) and the TV series based on it.

There's just one problem.

People don't commonly eat these crabs. There's no evidence – beyond Huxley's hypothetical – that fisherman ever sorted and saved any of them. They don't grow much larger, measured across the carapace, than 2 cm, or maybe an inch. That's not much meat, and awfully tedious picking to get at it.

Marine biologist Joel Martin dismissed the role of artificial selection in the appearance of faces on the backs of samurai crabs, showing that their grooves and ridges make room for internal organs and musculature.[4] In the end, the desire to see samurai on the back of crabs is nothing more than an instance of pareidolia, a human phenomenon in which our brains strive to make sense of patterns and abstractions and often come up with – surprise – human forms, especially faces. But the desire to explain those faces as a product of our own actions suggests something else at work.

In the Huxley/Sagan myth, Man (I use the gendered term purposefully) is a kind of minor farmer-god engaging in a form of accidental animal husbandry that brought out certain species traits and suppressed others in the crabs. If the Heike myth was, in the end, only speculative and eventually discountable, it nevertheless remains true that humans have tremendous impact on the lives of non-human animals. We insert ourselves everywhere, making the world more to our liking – and more to our likeness.

At the same time, we project our own insecurities onto creatures with motives to which we have little access. The notion of 'crab mentality' draws on the creature's observed behaviours to deride human foibles, possibly deriving from a Filipino adage: put one lone crab in a basket and he will figure out how to climb out. A dozen crabs, however, will pull the one that tries to escape back down into the basket. Roughly comparable to the phrase 'tall poppy syndrome' used in the United Kingdom, Australia and New Zealand (in fact, many societies use a similar aphorism), 'crab mentality' suggests bullying competition and self-defeating resentment. Let's hope it is only humans, and not some unfortunate crabs, that actually suffer from it.

The persistence of a certain set of characteristics appearing in myths, literature and popular culture involving crabs suggests that humans think they know crabs pretty well. Karkinos, Crios, Sebastian, Mr Krabs and their kin are full of personality, mixing qualities such as indefatigability and irritability – that is, what we sometimes call 'crabbiness'. When scientists consider personality among non-human animals, they usually focus on evaluating differences among individual members of a species according to their degree of activity level, sociability, aggression, boldness or shyness, and their tendencies to explore or avoid new experiences.[5]

But the consistent personality markers we attribute to crabs – their feistiness, doggedness and skittishness – may actually be species- (or family-) typical behaviours that serve purposes other than our assumptions. We might label an animal that darts towards shelter when a shadow passes overhead as prone to over-reaction, but for animals preyed on by birds, such a move is a reasonably prudent manoeuvre. Or we can curse a crab as pugnacious, but who can blame animals of any size for trying to put up a fight against someone who has trapped them in nets or who is about to toss them into a pot of boiling water? It's easy enough to accept that crabs, despite our legends, are not brave soldiers, sidekicks to the gods or other figures of our fantasies. But what are their lives like? What motivates their behaviours? What do they think or feel – or, to start closer to scratch, *do* they think and feel?

We might not expect sophisticated cognition from an animal whose brain consists of just a few fused ganglia, located on the

Oriana Poindexter, *Rock Crab*, 2019.

dorsal (top) side of the front of the carapace. At the risk of over-simplifying, the crab brain can be described as a cluster of nerves connecting to the oesophagus, eyestalks, eye muscles, optic nerves, antennae and smaller antennule. They also connect to oesophageal and stomatogastric ganglia, which comprise a relatively lengthy ladder or chain transmitting neural information between mouthparts and the digestive system. At the end of that ladder, crabs have thoracic ganglia, much larger than the nerve cluster that we call their brain. This cluster sends sensory data and muscle-controlling signals to and from the ventral (ground-facing) side, the anus and the legs. While the human nervous system is also distributed throughout the body, we tend to think of our brain as its seat, our command centre, a function that is more widely diffused in a crab. (Maybe we should say that the crab has more than one brain!) As biologist Patricia Backwell, who spends several months each year studying fiddler crabs on the coasts of Australia's Northern Territory, tells me, 'a crab's memory is in his legs.'

What kinds of memory, degree of sentience or capacities for decision-making and learning does a crab have, in her legs or elsewhere? We might say 'not much', if we want to measure against our own nervous system, which is crammed with a hundred billion neurons. (Neurons of various types transmit sensory data and control muscular movement. For comparison's sake, an African elephant has about a quarter as many neurons as a human; a dog, roughly 10 per cent of the elephant's neural load; a cockroach, about a million neurons; a crab, only about 100,000. The long-finned pilot whale, a large dolphin, has twice as many neocortical neurons as any human. The number of neurons it takes for animals to live their lives is, obviously, quite varied.)

Perhaps the most basic question about crab cognition involves the creature's capacity to experience pain and suffering. Utilitarian philosopher Jeremy Bentham (1748–1832) argued that when it comes to non-human animals and to understanding differences between us and them, we often ask the wrong questions: 'The question is not, Can they *reason*? nor, Can they *talk*? but Can they *suffer*?'[6] Many in the fishing and restaurant industries, and even home cooks, have long held that crabs (and lobsters) have such simple nervous systems that they do not feel pain. Some scientists agree and differentiate reflexive behaviour from anything that we as humans – and our closer relatives, the vertebrates – would call pain. In other words, if you toss a crab into a pot of boiling water and he tries to climb out, is that a simple reflex, or is the crab struggling against suffering? These perspectives mitigate concerns we should have about common techniques for shipping, storing and cooking these animals, for whom processing begins while they are still alive. (More on crab as a foodstuff in another chapter.) After all, if they don't seem to mind being kept on ice, why should we mind? They may mind quite a bit, but a cold environment has a sedating effect on crustaceans, so lack of evidence that they are in any discomfort can be blamed on dormancy. Likewise, they may suffer tremendously when boiled to death. We may simply not be aware of the signs of their suffering. Or we may choose to ignore them.

Increasingly, biologists are concluding from experimentation with live crustaceans that they may feel pain. But what is pain? How do we know that an action is not a simple reflex? The answer lies in what happens *after* a painful experience. When we touch a hot flame or surface, or get an electric shock, or some similar experience, we don't have to *decide* to move away from the uncomfortable stimulus. That's a reflex, specifically a withdrawal reflex, also known as nociception, in which a combination of sensory and motor neurons work together quickly to protect the organism, allowing us to pull back a hand, shift our weight, or otherwise evade a dangerous stimulus without thinking. No decision-making is required. Our nervous systems can do this, as can those of other vertebrates and invertebrates, including crabs.

A painful experience is different from one that provokes a reflex. Pain is a staged process, beginning with the nociceptive reflex, followed by feelings about having experienced the pain, and learned aversion to the stimulus. Barry Magee and Robert W. Elwood, who studied pain in crabs, call this an 'aversive negative affective state . . . that involves awareness, interpretation and long-term behavioural change'.[7] In their studies, crabs responded to painful stimulus in ways that indicated that they were aware of it, made memories of it and changed future behaviours to minimize the chance of re-experiencing it. A purely reflexive response does not lead to future behavioural change.

Magee and Elwood worked with *Carcinus maenas*, a swimming crab native to the eastern shores of the Atlantic Ocean from North Africa to Norway and the Baltic Sea, but widely invasive elsewhere. They are commonly known as European green crabs or shore crabs. They can survive in a range of environments but prefer habitats with hiding places like layered rocks or aquatic plant life. Taking advantage of this characteristic, Magee and Elwood placed shore crabs in tanks that included two dark shelters, knowing that the animals would prefer these spots to the rest of the well-lit tank – and, in the absence of negative stimuli, they found that the crabs would show strong bias for returning to the same shelter each time they were placed in the tank. Entering the tank, crabs tended to choose a shelter quickly. In one randomly chosen shelter, they would be allowed to rest quietly. If they chose the other, they received a 10-volt shock, which the researchers believed to be enough to provoke a response but below the threshold of causing significant damage. Nevertheless, a few crabs did autotomize when shocked (they shed a leg or portion of a leg, which would likely grow back in future moults, albeit at some cost, given the energy required and increased vulnerability while missing limbs). Most crabs exited the shock shelter – if not after one shock, certainly after repeated shocks. When retested, some refused to enter either shelter, even though that meant that they had to remain in the brighter parts of the tank. Crabs that weren't shocked their first time in the tank went back consistently to the same shelter in a second trial. Importantly, crabs that were shocked fought this bias and learned to choose the other shelter. Researchers were careful to eliminate anything in the tank that might provide a visual or olfactory clue about which shelter would lead to a shock, and they placed crabs into the tank in different orientations each time, so that the crabs had to do more than simply learn to turn right or left to reach the safer shelter. The crabs had to remember which shelter was the source of their discomfort. Did Magee and Elwood prove that crabs feel pain? They drew cautious but specific conclusions: crabs are capable

Crab wired prior to pain test.

Chasmagnathus granulata, Plate 100 in *Grapsoid Crabs of America* by Mary J. Rathbun (1918).

of 'swift avoidance learning, which is a key criterion/expectation for pain experience'.

Another team of researchers who had previously studied crab memory and learning in laboratory settings relocated their tests to the field, where they could encounter *Chasmagnathus granulatus* in its natural habitats on mudflats south of Buenos Aires. (This crab is now sometimes known as *Neohelice granulata*, since another author issued a paper arguing that it constitutes its own unique genus.[8]) The Argentinian carcinologists, led by María del Valle Fathala, knew that these crabs would make rapid bee-lines to their individual burrows if they believed that a predatory bird was nearing. They rigged up a motorized device that allowed them to pass a rectangle over a section of the mudflat. Using video cameras, they observed and recorded how the crabs responded to the passing shadow. They could distinguish 'unprovoked retreats' from 'provoked retreats', because in the former, a crab might stop en route to perform other tasks, move deeper into the burrow and stay inside longer. In provoked retreats, crabs hid just beyond the entrance, as if to monitor when danger would pass so they could continue with normal activities. With repeated exposure to the shadow produced by what they called the 'Visual Danger Stimulus', crabs behaved in ways that suggested that they were 'desensitized' to the presence of the object in their environment – and, importantly, when it was presented at regular intervals they learned to change the duration of their above-ground explorations to avoid it. Fathala et al. were confident that they had demonstrated that crabs had the capacity for learning and short-term memory in the field, under more complex conditions than traditional lab experiments. A follow-up experiment, in which they sought to determine if the crabs retained memories of the experience a full 24 hours after initial testing, suggested that they continued to alter their behaviours in ways provoked the previous day: evidence of longer-term learning.[9]

Are the crabs really learning, or is being 'desensitized' to a visual stimulus actually something else, a reflex of sorts? To be sure, living creatures are capable of adapting to sensory experiences, such as changes in light, temperature or an odour that might have initially been stimulating. Likewise, the body can just give up responding to a repeated sensation if fatigue sets in. But that's not what happened to the *N. granulata* crabs in Fathala's study. Instead, they *habituated* to a stimulus that initially appeared potentially predatory and merited a self-preserving dash towards home. Habituation is a form of learning; without it, we'd all be jumping out of our skins at every leaf-rustling breeze. With repeated exposures, the crabs tended to realize that this shadow didn't present any real danger.[10] Similarly, females in a population of *Uca vomeris* (the southern calling fiddler crab) in Queensland, Australia, subjected to a 'dummy predator', discerned after multiple exposures that they could ignore it. (When a similar dummy was run on a line over the crabs from a different direction, they made 'home runs' towards their burrows, reading the shadow as a new possible threat.) Males didn't habituate so easily; researchers suggested that their more brightly coloured claws might make them more vulnerable to predation, and that while females may enjoy relatively peaceful access to their burrows, males vie over burrows more frequently. The greater their need to protect themselves and their homes, the slower one would expect them to be able to habituate: that is, the more discerning they would be about when to engage in 'an active suppression of response' to a stimulus that could plausibly cause harm.

Another team of researchers, led by Ross J. Roudez, then a student at Rutgers University in Newark, New Jersey, tested crabs' retention of learned behaviours after a longer interval, a full ten days. This particular study added a twist, seeking to show how quickly two different species learned to locate a new food source. Planting a mussel among plastic greenery in a tank, researchers recorded the time it took for European green crabs and blue crabs (*Callinectes sapidus*) to find the food. Green crabs performed impressively. In each of five successive tries they improved their 'capture time' significantly, and they continued to improve when retested the next day, indicating that they remembered where to look. Only one of twenty green crabs performed at a much lower

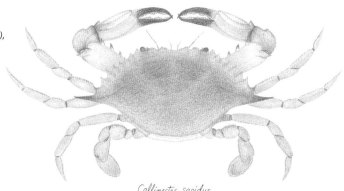

Tanya L. Rogers, *Callinectes sapidus (Atlantic Blue Crab),* 2012, coloured pencil.

Callinectes sapidus

level. In contrast, fewer than half of the blue crabs managed to find the mussel within the allotted time, and in repeated attempts most did not improve their 'capture time'. Retested after ten days, green crabs captured the food as quickly as they had during earlier tests. Blue crabs were nearly back to square one.[11] In other words, green crabs proved themselves quick learners with good memories, while a large majority of blue crabs seemed to retain little information about how to locate the new food source over both the short and long terms: each trial was a blank slate for most of the blues.

Why would these researchers have sought to compare the learning skills of green and blue crabs? The choice was far from arbitrary. The blue crab's native habitats stretch along the Western Atlantic Ocean and the north coast of the Gulf of Mexico; they are important to both commercial and recreational fishing industries in these regions, with the largest catches in Maryland and Louisiana. The invasive European green crabs are native to Europe, but by the time this study was published in 2007 they were well established from Maine to Maryland, elbowing their way into blue crab territory. Roudez et al. wondered why green crabs are such successful invaders. There are, surely, many reasons. For one, during larval stages, young crabs (of many types) are easily trapped in ships' ballast water, which may be released far from where it is taken up. Green crabs also have a relatively high tolerance for varying degrees of salinity and a wide range of temperatures, and they are willing to add new foods to their diets. In other words, they are robustly adaptable to new environments. Maybe, researchers conjectured, they are also more intelligent than the average crab.

The results of this study support the theory that learning and memory skills enhance adaptability, amounting to competitive

Larval stages of the common shore crab (*C. maenas*), from W. T. Calman, *Life of Crustacea* (1911).

Yashima Gakutei, *Crabs Near the Water's Edge*, c. 1830, polychrome woodblock print (surinomo), ink and colour on paper.

advantage over species with lesser skills. But, as scientific attention to personality differences among individuals within a species have shown, each member of a species is not a carbon copy of the next. We should expect variability among the quick-learning green crabs, as well as among the slower-to-catch-on blue crabs. Interestingly, a few blue crabs performed better than most in this study, finding the mussel just a little bit quicker in each successive attempt, suggesting that some learning was taking place, slowly but surely – albeit nowhere near the pace of the green crabs. This may mean that blue crabs are not incapable of learning, simply that with a history of ready food sources and little competition, they have never had to do it. Time will tell if, with increasing competition for resources from the green crabs, the blue crabs are able to adapt: that is, if they are able to learn to learn.

What do such studies tell us about how crabs think? We can only infer the affective states of animals that cannot describe their experiences to us. We may have been quick to judge, to create so many stories about crabs characterizing them as blundering nervous wrecks and quarrelsome pests. They remain, even in the experience of a Maryland waterman like Grant Corbin, inscrutable, furtive, sidelong. But it might pay to consider that any animal that can learn to discriminate between choices with good and not-so-good outcomes may not be so simple after all.

4 If It Walks Like a Crab . . .

'You will never make the crab walk straight.'
Hierocles, in *Peace* by Aristophanes (c. 421 BCE)

In Aristophanes' play *Peace*, the oracle Hierocles invokes the crab to liken the near inevitability of war to the inexorably predictable behaviour of the crab. Just as humanity seems hardwired to lust for battle, the crab always walks sideways. It's a perfect metaphor, given our insistence that the sidelong gait is one of the defining characteristics of the crab. (Never mind that there are actually crabs that can and do swim, climb trees and walk forwards.) The sideways walk and hard shell are both so strongly associated with the crab that they inspired Robert De Niro's performance in a scene from *Taxi Driver* (dir. Martin Scorsese, 1976):

> 'I got the idea of making Travis move like a crab,' says De Niro. 'It's a hot sunny day. He's out of his cab, which is his protective shell – he's outside his element. He's all hot and dry, finally he breaks down. I got the image of a crab, moving awkwardly, sideways and back.'[1]

De Niro searched the animal world for inspiration, where he found the crab's most readily identified physical and behavioural traits: they are so prominent that we seem to believe them to contain the whole story of the crab, whose life script is written through and only through these constraints. In such a view of animal life, crabs (and their kin) operate as René Descartes saw them: as nothing more than automatons whose behaviours are fully mechanized – hardwired, we might say today. 'The animals lack a mind,' he wrote in a letter to a friend, and to another, 'They do not have the power to determine themselves.'[2]

This view is hopelessly outdated, say modern scientists. Non-human animals are capable of far more than reflexive behaviours: memory, learning, communication, the sensation of pain and even a range of emotions. It is easier to recognize these qualities in animals more like us – mammals, especially the apes – than the invertebrates. And in all animal species – including our own – there is uncertainty about how behaviours result from a mix of genetic histories and environmental conditions, including social experience. It's probably true that animals' capacity to 'determine themselves' varies along a spectrum, and if so, humans and our primate kin may be on one end, and our crab friends some distance away. But having a brain that consists of only a precious few ganglia does not stop crabs from engaging in complex, surprising and distinct sets of behaviours: behaviours that distinguish crabs from other animals, one crab species from another, and even members of the same species from each other.

Wind-up toy crab, made in Hong Kong.

What do crabs do all day, anyway? What do we know about the behaviour of crabs? How much *can* we know about these animals' lives? Why do we think of them as simple and their behaviours mechanistic – or complex, even enigmatic? After all, for better or worse, how we think of other animals always seems to be part of a conversation we are having with ourselves about what kind of animals *we* are.

Ceramic bowl, 2nd–4th century, Nasca, Peru.

All animals engage in behaviours – such as reproductive cycles, prey drive or hibernation – that aren't simply self-determined but are influenced by biology and instinct. For crabs and other arthropods, one such behaviour is the moult. Crabs moult multiple times during their lifespans, most frequently during larval stages, then several times as juveniles, and at much longer intervals (or not at all) as adults. A king crab, for example, can moult half a dozen times in its first year but only undergoes an annual moult by the time it reaches four years of age. Early in 2018, I went to the Scripps Institution of Oceanography in La Jolla, California, to meet an expert on crustacean biomechanics. When I arrived at Jennifer Taylor's office, I didn't need to see a room number. Her door was open, and on the wall behind her desk was a framed photo of a bright red crab. A west-facing window looked out onto the Pacific Ocean, surfers and the beach.

When I asked Taylor why she chose to study blue crabs and the moulting process, she answered matter-of-factly: in her profession, one's choices often depend on the availability of study objects. Blue crabs were plentiful not far from where she did her graduate work, at the University of North Carolina (though Chapel Hill itself is land-locked), and people at a local fishery were interested in helping her understand moulting. The market in soft-shells depends on good timing – knowing when to take crabs in the small window after their hard shells have been shed and before the new shell hardens. The more that crab fisheries can learn about how to identify a crab that is about to moult, the better their harvest. In the first twelve hours after a moult, the crabs are what the seafood industry calls 'peelers', a seasonal treat popular among consumers who don't want to bother picking crab. Often the whole crab is fried and served between slices of bread; there's no shell to remove, only eyes, gills and the abdominal apron to snip away.

There is obvious commercial value in this kind of research, but is there scientific interest? Taylor grinned and glowed with excitement. When a blue crab moults, she says, it can increase its body

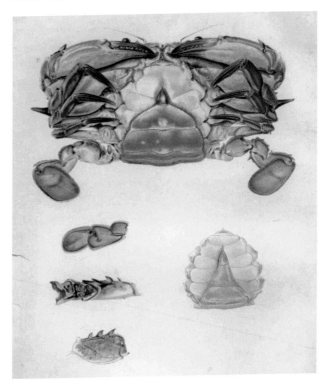

Colouration of the crab in moulting stages, plate xlvii from E. P. Churchill, Jr, *Life History of the Blue Crab* in *Bulletin of the United States Bureau of Fisheries*, XXXVI (1917–18).

All arthropods – not only crustaceans – moult. Young horseshoe crab moult, dorsal view.

mass by 40 per cent. Taylor was fascinated by the processes that allow for such a sudden growth spurt. How does an animal spend much of its energy preparing to moult, moulting and recovering from the moult? In describing how taxing the process is for some species, her enthusiasm was contagious – and why shouldn't it be? Moulting is a dramatic process. When most crabs moult, they begin secreting layers of a new cuticle that will become their new shells, and drink large amounts of water that put pressure on their exoskeleton, eventually cracking it. These crabs then slip out of their old carapaces (ecdysis), often leaving behind perfectly intact and detailed shells, like abandoned suits of clothing. (Some land crabs fill up with air instead of water during the moult.) An old shell, once hard and layered, reveals itself as a delicate sheath, once armour-like, now ghostly. After a half day or so, as chitin, proteins and calcium carbonate accumulate, a crab's new shell enters a 'paper' stage, during which it is tough but not yet rigid. Within days, newly hardened, the moulting process ends . . . for the time being.

Moulting requires huge amounts of energy and renders a crab vulnerable to predators (including humans fishing for 'peelers') until a new shell hardens. The way that crabs and other crustaceans moult is unlike that of many other arthropods, requiring a structural shift between two typically distinct types

Flame-backed
fiddler crab
(*Uca flammula*),
Northern Territory,
Australia.

of skeleton. Most animals have, throughout their lifetimes, either a rigid skeleton (internally, for vertebrates, in contrast to invertebrates with exoskeletons) or a hydrostatic skeleton (found in soft-bodied animals such as jellyfish, earthworms and anemones), in which movement is a coordinated interplay of musculature, fluid and an external membrane. Blue crabs and others that fill themselves with water during the moult are not only using the water to crack the old shell and make room for growth in the new shell – they are gaining a temporary hydrostatic skeleton for the period of time that they lose their rigid exoskeleton.[3] It is a temporary transmogrification rarely seen in the animal world. And yet, despite how complex the behaviour of moulting is, and the fact that huge numbers of crabs may moult at roughly the same time, the process is experienced individually. A wide range of other crab behaviours are more social in nature, involving other crabs, and sometimes members of other species.

One of the most charming social behaviours in the crab world just might be the fiddler crab's wave. Fiddlers aren't hard to find

– not in coastal areas, anyway. There are about a hundred known species of the genus *Uca* distributed throughout the world, wherever there are salt marshes or mangrove forests. While modest in size – 5 cm (2 in.) across the shell or less – one of the male's claws is always larger than the other, sometimes outlandishly so, while females' claws are relatively small and symmetrical. Fiddlers are filter feeders and spend much of their time outside of their burrows using their small claw (or, in the case of females, both claws) to bring mud into their mouths, sieving out nutritious algae, fungi and detritus from local plant life to ingest. They skitter in and out of burrows as they assess the level of threat posed by birds passing overhead or by stomping humans and our looming shadows. Sometimes, males wave their big claws in a vigorous attempt to attract a mate.

Two fiddler species, *Uca pugnax* and *Uca pugilator*, live in densely populated and adjacent habitats in marshy estuaries from Cape Cod to the Gulf Coast, and like many crabs they have their own unique repertoire of behaviours. On Great Island, in

Porcelain fiddler crabs (*Uca annulipes*), Inhaca island, Mozambique.

Wellfleet, Massachusetts, *U. pugnax*, the Atlantic marsh fiddler crab, flourishes in the mud flats that dot the salt marshes. Their olive carapaces blend well into the mud, but the males' blue streaks can gleam, and their large claws, whitish or yellowish, easily catch the eye. Their abundance is a marvel. At times, it seems as if the entire ground is alive, on the move. It is also perforated with countless holes that lead to the crab's single-occupancy burrows. Just beyond the intertidal zone, the sand fiddler *U. pugilator* can be seen, though not in quite such large numbers. Louis Bosc, a French botanist and zoologist who travelled around Charleston, North Carolina, in the late eighteenth century, named it the 'little pugilist' (not to be confused with the boxer crabs of the genus *Lybia)*. Bosc seems to have found these fiddlers particularly scrappy. Males will readily grapple with one another in fights, usually over territory: the sand fiddler sometime uses his major claw to drum noisily, while the marsh fiddler uses his big claw in a seemingly choreographed mating ritual.

It is not unusual for males of many species to engage in spectacular performances of one kind or another when seeking to attract mates. Some sing, some dance, some show off their skills in providing food, or they engage in some other display. It is also not unusual for groups of animals to act in synchrony. For example, fish or birds may swim or fly in apparently coordinated movements known as adaptive synchrony. Acting as a unit, they may confuse or put off predators that would have an easy time catching isolated prey. In contrast, in incidental synchrony, animals engage in the same behaviour at the same time, not to blend in but rather to 'stand out'.[4] This is the case among some species that vocalize to attract mates – whoever calls first, finest, loudest or longest wins the sexual competition. There are few known instances of synchronous visual display as a mating tactic, except among some species of fiddler crab.

When some fiddlers seek mates, it is the male that goes looking, and they hook up without display of any kind. Then there are 'female searching' species, where females take strolls through areas with concentrations of males to search for potential mates. In these cases, males wave their large claw to appeal to the searching female. According to Pat Backwell, females tend to choose mates with the largest claws, the fastest waves and, importantly, 'wave leadership'. That is, when members of a group of males notice a female nearby, the one who starts waving just a fraction of a second before the others is most likely to win a mate. Even so, if a male doesn't see a female approaching his territory – if she is out of his range of vision – but other males in the area do see her and start waving, he'll do his best to catch up, waving with his fellow males. In these cases, the male is a copycat, not directly cued by the sight of a female to start waving, but able to read his peers' actions and join them in waving, a form of communication using 'socially acquired information' with considerable complexity.[5]

Male banana fiddler crabs (*Uca mjoebergi*) waving, Darwin Harbour, Australia.

Backwell and her students observe *Austruca mjoebergi*, also known as the banana fiddler crab because of the male's huge yellow claw. In Canberra, over coffee in a bustling café on the campus of the Australian National University, where she is a professor in the Research School of Biology, Backwell tells me that she strongly prefers conducting field research, rather than taking animals into the lab, and that she is careful to design experiments that disrupt the crabs' lives as little as possible. Studying female preferences in mate selection, her team even minimized the number of crabs involved by creating small, motorized crabs, each capped off with a bright yellow plaster claw. They commanded the robotic crabs to wave in unison, and other patterns. Observing the females approach the robots, which they must have presumed to be males, Backwell concluded that the leading wave is a favoured 'signal', but that if a group of males waving in synchrony lacks a leader, a female will look for another good sign, like the largest claw – perhaps not her ideal mate, but one with still impressive attributes.

Male banana fiddlers may use their claws to signal their powers of speed, strength and leadership, but some crabs engage in behaviours that require objects other than their own body parts. Until well past the middle of the twentieth century, scientists and non-scientists alike believed that one of the defining features of the human animal (or, as the literature of that era often said, 'man') is the ability to make and use tools. Indeed, our ancestors *Australopithecus garhi* and *Homo habilis* were shaping stones into Oldowan tools (basically, rocks intentionally broken to create a sharp edge) some 2.5 MYA. In *Man the Tool-maker*, Kenneth P. Oakley maintained that while chimpanzees had been observed 'improvising tools' when both materials and a significant reward were within their grasp, the mind of even a great ape could not engage in the abstract thinking required to *make* a tool for some 'imagined future eventuality'.[6] No planning, no preparation. Meanwhile, Jane Goodall was in Tanzania, gathering evidence indicating that some chimpanzees strip the leaves off branches that could then be used to dig or fish insects out of their mounds, and that others sharpen sticks with their teeth to use as spears when hunting small mammals, all of which seemed to require something that is hard to avoid calling a plan or preparation for future action.

Eventually, it became uncontroversial to note that a number of animals use tools in various ways, usually to obtain food or water, sometimes to create shelters – not only primates but sea otters, bottlenose dolphins, elephants, crows and ravens, and octopuses. Most of these species are already recognized as the cleverest problem-solvers of the non-human animal world. But the tiny brachyuran crabs of the genera *Polydectus* and *Lybia* make a regular practice of carrying tools in their unusually small claws. (For years, these crabs were recognized as the only tool-using invertebrates, but in 2009 scientists began to recognize the octopus as a pretty handy tool-user, too.[7]) As if that's not unusual enough, these 'tools' are living creatures, usually sea anemones, sometimes sponges, corals or nudibranchs. Accordingly, members of these species are often called 'boxing', 'boxer' or 'pom-pom' crabs, since they appear to be wearing hefty gloves or brandishing tufted pom-poms, like a cheerleader.

Boxer crabs aren't the only crabs that live in symbiotic relationships with individuals of other species. There are, for example, crabs of several different families that cling to sea whips (a 'soft coral', or Alcyonacea) or to 'hard' or 'stony' corals (the Scleractinia). These crabs eat mucus emitted by the corals and take shelter among them, while the corals enjoy some clawed protection from predators such as starfish.[8] But these arrangements are much more conventionally mutualistic, with each animal remaining

Lybia leptochelis, holding a pair of sea anemones.

somewhat autonomous while benefitting from their entangled lives.

Writing in 1880, Karl Mobius and his colleagues noted the unusual behaviour of anemone-carrying when describing *Melia* (now *Lybia*) *tessellata* specimens from the Indian and Pacific Oceans. They characterized the relationship between the boxer crabs and the anemones (referred to as 'actinians') as an example of commensalism. In contemporary usage, commensalism indicates a relationship beneficial to one species and neutral to another. But he described an arrangement of mutual benefit: the crab allows the anemone to gather food, then uses a walking leg to take the food away from his passenger and deliver it to his own mouth. Meanwhile, the anemone takes a ride to new food sources that it would not be able to reach if attached to a rock or empty shell.[9] Even so, the boxer might get more out of the arrangement than the anemone. During a research trip to the Hawaiian Islands in 1905, James Edwin Duerden of Rhodes University College in Grahamstown (now Makhanda, South Africa) observed that the crab directs the anemones towards any perceived threat. They make fine defensive weapons, given that their tentacles sport the stinging cells known as cnidocytes or nematocysts.

Duerden collected some of these Hawaiian boxer crabs – *Melia tessellate* – and their anemones, to try to learn more about their relationships. The crabs were very reluctant to give up their anemones, but Duerden saw that if offered a larger anemone, a crab might let go of a smaller anemone and take the larger as its pom-pom instead. He identified the anemones that the boxers carry as members of the genera *Bunodeopsis* or *Sagartia*, or in some cases, one of each. When he pried one away from a crab, leaving her chela empty, he found that within fifteen minutes she would 'tear a single actinian in two in order to provide each claw with a polyp'.[10]

That the crab literally forces one anemone to become two is remarkable. Tear many other creatures in half and you've got two pieces of a dead animal. But anemones belong to the phylum Cnidaria, which also includes jellyfish, coral and sea fans, which can generally reproduce either sexually or asexually. While Duerden was aware of the behaviour over a hundred years ago, an in-depth study seems to have occurred only in the twenty-first century. Yisrael Schnytzer collected *Lybia leptochelis* on beaches in Eliat, Israel, at the northernmost tip of the Gulf of Aqaba, which juts like a rabbit's ear off the Red Sea. While *L. tessellata* is often said to have the appearance of stained glass, *L. leptochelis* looks more like a ragged crumb of fried tempura batter.[11] Collecting them was no small task. Besides being tiny, Schnytzer has reported that they are incredibly difficult to spot and scurry with startling speed if a rock they are hiding under is moved. Their elusiveness may contribute to the relative dearth of scientific writing about these creatures.[12]

All the crabs, including juveniles, held anemones – believed to be an unidentified species in the genus *Alicia* – in each chela. To test how crabs would respond if left without their symbiots, researchers removed one or both anemones from some of the crab's claws, a painstaking process that sometimes required sedation using magnesium chloride. Seventeen of 22 crabs left with one anemone used their foremost walking legs to cut it in half within six days. When a crab deprived of both anemones was put in an environment with a crab holding two anemones, three-quarters of them picked a fight that ended when the anemone-less crab made off with all or part of one of the other crab's anemone.[13] However fierce, none of the fights resulted in injuries to either crab. Obviously, anemone-less crabs were intensely motivated to obtain new anemones, either by forcing one to clone or by theft from a peer.

The boxer crab doesn't just steal when lacking an anemone. It also steals food from its own anemones. Elsewhere, Schnytzer and

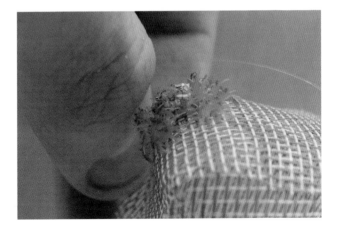

L. leptochelis with anemones, held by researcher.

his collaborators name this behaviour 'kleptoparasitism' – that is, exploitation of a symbiot through food theft. So much for mutualism. In their lab, these researchers freed some anemones from their boxer hosts, allowed them to eat at will and watched them grow an astonishing 177 per cent in just six weeks. Meanwhile, anemones held by crabs shrunk some 38 per cent. The impact of food theft by crabs on the anemones was so extreme that Schnytzer et al. referred to it as a '"Bonsai" effect', in which the anemone is starved to maintain a body size convenient for the crab to hold and manipulate.[14] *Lybia* may look like boxers with outsized gloves, or cheerleaders with tentacled pom-poms, but they may actually be quite strict gardeners, harvesting dinner and shooing away predators with tools that just happen to be alive. No wonder Schnytzer says that when he discusses his research interests with people who are not marine biologists, they tend

L. leptochelis as bonsai artist: holding anemones whose feeding the crab has controlled, next to an anemone freed from a boxer crab and allowed to eat at will.

to say, "'That's interesting, but what's the practical benefit?' "Nothing", he always replies, "they're just really amazing."'[15]

Boxer crabs may uniquely carry other tiny sea creatures in their forelegs, to intimidate potential predators or to exploit as food-gatherers, but many kinds of crabs also engage in close and controlling relationships with other marine animals and plants. These brachyurans hail from the superfamily Majoidea. Members of two of its five families, the Majidae and Oregoniidae, are sometimes called spider crabs for their long and spindly legs. And some of them earn other nicknames thanks to a behavioural quirk. They are the so-called 'decorator' crabs, also known as Velcro crabs, dresser crabs or little seaweed crabs, because they place algae, sponges and other sea-life on their carapaces, which have sticky hook-like hairs that help their adornments hang on. Members of the family Homolidae engage in a similar behaviour, but through a different mechanism: their fifth pair of walking legs can bend in such a way that the creature can hold a sponge, coral or urchin on the rear portion of its carapace. Their nickname is the 'carrier' or 'porter' crab.

Clearly, decorators are manipulating objects, like tool users, but decorations are not exactly tools: typically, scientists define a tool as an object detached from the animal using it. In contrast, a decorator is 'an organism that . . . accumulates and retains environmental material that becomes attached to the exterior of the decorator'.[16] It may seem fanciful to say that an animal 'decorates' him- or herself. When a pig wallows to coat herself in mud, she gains a practical layer of protection from sun and pests. Some insects build something like shields from their own excrement, random detritus or, in the case of the assassin bug, dead ants, all probably to discourage predators. In other words, there is usually some function beyond the aesthetic. In the case of decorator crabs, it has long been assumed that the purpose of their decorations is

Decorator crab, illustrated in Charles Frederick Holder, *Along the Florida Reef* (1892).

94

camouflage. The gardens carried on their backs don't seem to give decorator crabs a competitive advantage in mating; they only occasionally draw on them as a food source. So what else could account for this behaviour?

In a 1913 publication, H. C. Stevens asks the obvious questions about the decorating behaviour: *how* do they do it ('by what means or instruments are the foreign bodies made to adhere'); *what* prompts the behaviour ('by the action of what stimuli'); and *why* do they do it ('what end is sought, what purpose is served')? But no sooner has Stevens asked the questions than he collapses the third into the second, arguing that 'the crab seeks no end and carries out no purpose.' A purposeful action, he argues, would be possible only if the crab possessed some 'consciousness', which can be nothing more than the illusion of the 'anthropomorphizing human observer'.[17] Instead, according to Stevens, only the first two questions are relevant, and he set out to identify the stimulus that produces the response of decorating.

Decorator crab (*Oregonia gracilis*) with yellow sponges on its shell.

The standing literature on the subject, Stevens reminds us, was divided on the question of *how* the crab comes to have plant and animal life attached to its shell. Some experts had already described the crab as 'planting out' these ornaments. Posterior walking legs rotate and bend to place algae and such. Others claimed that the crabs 'permit all sort of foreign bodies' to attach themselves to their shells, requiring us to recognize modes of both 'active' and 'passive' decoration.[18] Either way, the result is ornamentation so dense that 'when moving it seems as if a small forest of sea-weed were being transplanted to another locality'.[19] That takes care of the first question – *how* the crab decorates its shell. But what brings on this behaviour, and why is one ornament chosen over another?

Stevens didn't exactly settle the question of what induces decorating, but, as prior research had also claimed, *seeing* a bit of seaweed or (in the lab) scraps of paper wasn't sufficient stimulus. The crabs were more likely to decorate using materials they had brushed up against, suggesting that tactile stimulation is important. Stevens tested this hypothesis in an experiment coldly indifferent to the fate of the crabs brought into his lab: they were blinded, 'by cutting off the eye stalks close to the orbit by a pair of scissors'.[20] The result? Sightlessness did not inhibit decorating.

Almost a century later, the function of decorating still seems a mystery. John Stachowicz and Mark E. Hay note that what little research has been done in this area usually frames decorating as 'visual camouflage', meaning that adornments would make the crab less visible to predators because they decorate with locally abundant sea-life, making them blend into their surroundings.[21] They chose to study *Libinia dubia*, or the long-nosed spider crab, which could be easily found on the shores of Morehead City, near the University of North Carolina's Institute of Marine Sciences. Only juveniles of this species regularly decorate; adults are

generally too large for local fish to grasp in their mouths, making them far less vulnerable to predation. In other words, once decorating to discourage predators is no longer necessary, individuals stop doing it.

These juvenile spider crabs turned out to be picky decorators. In both the lab and in their natural habitat, they strongly preferred to decorate with the brown alga *Dictoya menstrualis*, a type of seaweed that contains chemicals repellent to omnivorous pinfish, which gladly eat other seaweeds and small crabs lacking 'chemically defended' decorations. Instead of visual camouflage, then, their decorations serve as chemical camouflage – a kind of defensive weapon, even. Not all decorators choose toxic decorations, but for this particular population, in this locality, the mysterious function of this unusual behaviour seems a little less mysterious.

Decorator crab (*O. gracilis*), Monterey, California.

I would be foolish to generalize from this one study. At least seven hundred different crab species decorate, most from Majoidea. And not all nine hundred species of Majoidea decorate, though some three-quarters of them do. In *L. dubia*, only juveniles decorate, abandoning the practice as they grow. In *Camposcia retusa*, size doesn't matter; this spider-decorator crab decorates regardless of how large. When Danielle Dixson of the University of Delaware and an international team of collaborators sought to study decorating behaviours in this species, they noticed that in the wild, these crabs tended not to decorate their chelipeds and first walking legs, but heavily decorated the second through fifth pairs of legs, and placed only small decorations on their carapaces. (Other species tend to decorate most heavily towards the front, hiding their rostrum and antennae.) *C. retusa* followed the same pattern in the lab, whether they were given natural materials or polyester pom-poms, like those used in handicrafts, whose bright green and red threads seemed to clownishly mock the idea that decorating helps a crab blend into her environment. They also found that when offered shelters, the crabs decorated less, apparently since they had a place to hide. And not having over-ornamented their shells helped them fit into sheltering nooks and crannies.

H. C. Stevens seemed resigned, in 1913, to giving up on 'why' questions pertaining to decorator crabs. Some of the rest of us seem to wonder about little else. Still, most of us know what we know about crabs from the ways they behave when we encounter them in their own habitats, in live seafood markets, or in aquaria. We know that most of them tend to walk sideways, that many of them will hide under rocks or dash into burrows at the slightest disturbance. We might be aware that crabs moult, if we've encountered empty shells on a beach or in a fish tank, or if we've found a fried soft-shell crab on our dinner plates. A closer look, if you're wandering, say, the shores of Cape Cod or northern Australia, reveals that some crabs perform impressive displays to attract prospective mates. But much of what we know about behaviours taking place among species less familiar to most of us we owe to generations of marine biologists who have looked closely at crabs of various kinds going about their daily lives, making their livings, solving their problems.

Some of these animals' solutions to problems of the everyday are so complex that it's hard not to believe that, if not as individuals, then at least as species, they have done much to determine themselves. In that respect, they may not be so different from us after all.

5 A Deadly Catch?

But I love to feel events overlapping each other,
crawling over one another like wet crabs in a basket.
Lawrence Durrell, *Balthazar* (1958)

Occasionally, people who love to eat crab go to ridiculous lengths to satisfy their appetites. In 2011, after a man took the last eight crab legs from an all-you-can eat buffet in East Lampeter Township, Pennsylvania, another man punched him repeatedly in the face. At the assailant's trial, the victim testified, 'I wish I had just given him my crab legs.'[1] Early in 2019, people who had been waiting for a restaurant in Huntsville, Alabama, to replenish the crab legs on its $10.58 spread clashed over who should get first pick of the fresh supply. According to an off-duty police officer trying to eat when the fight broke out, customers did battle with tongs taken from the buffet, duelling like fencers – or, perhaps, competing crabs. Both incidents resulted in arrests, and in the latter case, the *New York Post* couldn't resist calling the unruly diners 'crabby customers'.[2]

You'd think they were fighting over caviar, lobster or a non-seafood extravagance like truffles. Caviar is expensive by any measure. Beluga or Ossetra roe costs thousands of dollars per kilogram (as do truffles), and the sturgeons that the most valuable roe comes from are so overharvested that the Convention on International Trade in Endangered Species of Wild Fauna and Flora (CITES) regulates their trade. Over a century ago, lobster was a common downmarket meal in coastal New England, but given the fragility of their meat and the high cost of shipping live

West Coast crabs, Dungeness and snow, at an East Coast grocery store.

lobsters to market, lobster tail can be an elegant and exclusive treat. Even the casual lobster roll, ubiquitous throughout coastal New England, is expensive compared to most other sandwiches. Caviar and lobster are associated with fancy restaurants and special occasions, but they aren't the only kinds of seafood that can be pricey.

Crabmeat goes to market despite fluctuating wild supplies, dauntingly difficult labour to fish and prepare it, and risks to both workers and consumers from crab allergens and other toxins they may carry. And it is big business. The global trade in crab accounted for about 285,600 tonnes of imports in just the first nine months of 2018, down slightly from 296,100 tonnes in the same three quarters of 2017 (that's nearly 650 million lb, or 295 million kg, of crab). Russia and China are leading exporters; the United States, China, the Republic of Korea and Japan import the most crab.[3] Diners at the world's top restaurants find crab on their plates. During seafood season at the restaurant Noma in Copenhagen, dishes may include boiled brown crab on flatbread, a serving of Arctic king crab which is both smoked and barbequed,

Oriana Poindexter, *Brown Box Crab, Long Beach*, 2015, from the series *Fish Market Chronicles*.

and a crab salad garnished with edible flowers, all part of an
eighteen-course tasting menu that costs 2,500 Danish kroner
(about $375, or £290) per person.[4] Elsewhere, crab occupies a less
fancified culinary niche. At national and international chain
restaurants like Red Lobster, Bubba Gump's or Joe's Crab Shack,
where a combination platter of Dungeness, snow and king crab
for one diner costs $37.99 (£30), crab is one of the most expensive
items on the menu. But these aren't fine-dining experiences. They
are casual franchises vaguely reminiscent of seaside authenticity.
Hired hands – crab pickers – may do much of the work before
crabmeat goes to market, fresh, frozen or canned, for use in soups,
salads, crab Louie, rangoon, crab cakes and other dishes. Crab
served whole requires diners to crack shells with a mallet or a crab

A crab shack in
the Wharf district
of Washington, DC.

Recipes from the first company in the United States to can crab meat, c. 1903.

cracker, and to pick morsels of meat out of tubular legs and curved claws, often while wearing a bib.

Fishing for and eating crab is hardly a new phenomenon. Perhaps the earliest proof that shellfish was part of early *Homo sapiens* diets, and those of our immediate hominid ancestors, has been found in caves at Pinnacle Point, on the southern coast of South Africa, which contain the remains of meals estimated to be 164,000 years old.[5] While reports on that discovery don't mention crab, there is evidence that early modern humans migrated from what is now South Africa, up the east coast of the continent, eventually into Asia and Europe. At least some of those humans ate crabs. Robert C. Walter led an international team of scientists who found hand axes and other tools from about 125,000 years ago on a Pleistocene reef on the coast of the Red Sea in Eritrea. Among the tools, they found the shells of oysters, other molluscs and 'big brachyuran crabs', all edible, all part of some long-ago meals.[6]

In other words, as long as there have been humans living along coastlines, crab has been a part, more or less, of human diets. Archaeological evidence shows that prehistoric Britons caught crab using baskets, and that Native Americans living along what is now the U.S. mid-Atlantic coast ate crabs regularly since at least 3000 BCE.[7] Cookbooks dating to the seventeenth century contain recipes for fried and stuffed crab dishes, as well as how to prepare recently moulted 'soft-shell' crabs, instructions for making crab croquettes or patties now known as crab cakes, and creamed or scalloped crab (crab 'dip').[8]

While fresh crab was available fresh only along coastlines, new methods of preserving food dating to the early nineteenth century paved the way for the introduction of all kinds of canned foods in markets far away from their points of origin. In the United States, canneries, many launched by manufacturers trained in Britain, packaged oysters in New York, salmon in northern California and lobster in Maine. But it was not until James McMenamin established a factory in Hampton, Virginia, sometime in the mid- to late 1870s, that 'tinned' crab became a successful product line, and gave the town its nickname: Crabtown.[9] Nevertheless, professional and home cooks in regions where fresh crab is available tend to avoid canned varieties. Pasteurized crabmeat packaged in plastic containers, which require refrigeration and have shorter shelf lives than steel cans, tends to have better flavour and texture – at least according to tips published to help consumers sort through alternatives to fresh Dungeness and rock crab when an algae bloom closed California fisheries in 2015. The algae create a neurotoxin called domoic acid that can produce severe shellfish poisoning in humans and other mammals.[10]

The delicacy of fresh crabmeat – so sweet, so perishable – and its scant availability away from coastal catches bolster its symbolic valence. Crabs appear among other foods in sixteenth- and seventeenth-century Dutch still-life paintings, suggesting that

McMenamin Crab Packing plant and fleet, c. 1900. Hand-line crabbers fished from log canoes.

Clara Peeters,
*Still-life with Crab,
Shrimps and
Lobster*, c. 1635–40,
oil on wood.

they were an extravagance worth showing off, alongside gleaming glassware and silver serving dishes. But these paintings did more than boast about their Golden Age collectors' riches and good taste. Known as *vanitas*, they also offered allegories of the fragility and transience of worldly wealth and pleasures, told in arrangements of seafood prone to spoilage, fruit on the verge of rot, half-drunk glasses of wine, timepieces and bones. Painters from other parts of Northern Europe continued to create versions of *vanitas*, occasionally including a crab, well into the nineteenth century. Later, around 1887–9, Vincent van Gogh completed two paintings of crabs that suggest modern, stripped-down versions of the genre, probably more influenced by Japanese painters and printmakers than by the Dutch masters. Van Gogh would have seen watercolours of marine subjects by Katsushika Hokusai (1760–1849) and others in *Le Japon artistique*, an illustrated magazine.

Willem Claesz.
Heda, *Breakfast
with a Crab*, 1648,
oil on canvas.

Katshushika Hokusai, *Crab and Rice Plant*, 19th century, woodblock print (surimono), ink and colour on paper.

Hokusai's crabs are vibrant but feather-light in marine settings. Van Gogh's are exercises in dense colour – weighty, isolated still-life objects. A meal seems the furthest thing from either artist's mind.

Wherever crab fisheries are big employers, the industry forms a significant economic sector, and the meat plays a part in local cuisine. For locals and tourists alike, crab is a source of local pride and identity. Communities celebrate any number of crabs – stone crab in Florida; blue crab from the Chesapeake Bay, the Gulf Coast or the Carolinas; Dungeness from the Pacific Northwest; brown crab from the coasts of the United Kingdom; blue manna (or sand) crab from the South Pacific and Indian Oceans; and in festivals, from the St Tammany Crab Festival in Slidell, Louisiana, to the Mandurah Crab Fest in Western Australia. The State of Maryland's Office of Tourism even promotes the Maryland Crab and Oyster Trail to tourists seeking to sample restaurants and markets featuring local shellfish throughout the state.

Other festivals seek primarily local participants. Every August in Wivenhoe, a picturesque village in Essex, England, a crabbing

competition celebrates the pastime of crabbing in the River Colne.
Some crabbers come armed with proper nets and baskets. Others,
especially children, simply tear a bit of bacon or white bread from
their lunchtime sandwiches, tie it to a string and toss it into the
waters. The crabs in the Colne and other connected waterways
aren't much good for eating, so they are nearly always thrown
back in. One can imagine that many of them are old pros at this
game of being caught and re-caught. I am even told that where
fine-dining gastropubs have cropped up riverside, the crabs have
developed a taste for prosciutto and focaccia instead of humbler
bait. On the day of the Wivenhoe Crabbing Competition, the
crabber who catches the largest crab, regardless of its culinary
preferences, goes home with a £25 prize and a trophy. The crabs,
by and large, go back into the river.

Vincent van Gogh,
Two Crabs, 1889,
oil on canvas.

Not all populations seek out crabs and other crustaceans as a source of food. In fact, many purposely avoid shellfish of all or some kinds. (Full disclosure: I'm crabmeat-avoidant. In my experience, there is nothing like getting to know an animal, reading and writing about it, to take it off the menu.) In Judaism, those who follow Kashrut, the Jewish dietary rules, eat only foods deemed kosher (derived from the Hebrew word *kashér*, meaning 'fit' or 'proper'), and avoid those that are treyf (derived from *treifah*, or non-kosher). Leviticus 11:9–11 spells out rules for determining if seafood is kosher or treyf:

> These you may eat of all that are in the waters. Everything in the waters that has fin and scales, whether in the seas or in the rivers, you may eat. But anything in the seas or the rivers that has not fins and scales, of the swarming creatures in the waters and of the living creatures that are in the waters, is an abomination to you. They shall remain an abomination to you; of their flesh you shall not eat, and their carcasses you shall have with abomination.[11]

A bucket of ready-to-eat crabs on the Jersey Shore, in Belmar, New Jersey.

Where this translation uses the term 'abomination', others opt for equally strong terms: 'detestable' or 'unclean'. Another of the Five Books of Moses, Deuteronomy 14:9 offers much the same advice: sea-life with both fins and scales are good to eat; those without one or both of these characteristics (shellfish, sharks, marine mammals, eel, catfish, sturgeon) are forbidden. Most Christians do not observe these laws, but many Seventh Day Adventists do avoid shellfish.

These major religions regulate consumption of shellfish as much as the meat of another frequently proscribed animal, the pig – but why? Exclusions might lie in practical concerns, if shellfish is seen as an easy vector for illness from contaminated waters or spoilage. There may also be an element of disgust provoked by the idea of eating animals that are omnivorous scavengers, 'bottom-feeders' whose diets are unknown. A sociological rationale might involve a group's creation of traditions that distinguish it from members of other groups. According to Mary Douglas, dietary laws also have symbolic value, functioning as 'allegories of virtues and vices'. Philo of Alexandria, for example, interpreted

Jewish dietary law as intentionally depriving the observant of some of the most delicious foods, to build both moral character and healthy bodies, like a kind of never-ending Lent:

> The lawgiver sternly forbade all animals of land, sea or air whose flesh is the finest and fattest, like that of pigs and scaleless fish, knowing that they set a trap for the most slavish of senses, the taste, and that they produced gluttony . . . gluttony begets indigestion, which is the source of all illnesses and infirmities.[12]

Even more convincingly, Douglas builds an argument for aspects of religious law that are 'arbitrary . . . disciplinary and not doctrinal'.[13] In other words, some rules are there simply so that we can practise obeying rules. In this analysis, engaging in a practice like avoiding shellfish (or pork, or following any number of other prohibitions) is a ritual conducted in recognition of a higher authority – an authority that doesn't have to explain rules, rational or irrational.

There are also those who have to avoid crabs and other shellfish, not because of religious prohibitions but because of allergies. While it is hard to pinpoint the exact number of people who suffer from shellfish allergies, some researchers estimate the figure at around 0.5 to 2.5 per cent of any given population. Shellfish allergies may be more common in some parts of the world than others and seem to be increasingly prevalent.[14] They are unusual in that many cases hit adults who have previously eaten crustaceans or molluscs safely, whereas most food allergies show up in childhood. And when a shellfish allergy hits, it is often severe. An allergic reaction can start with an itchy or swollen mouth, hives, gastrointestinal distress or trouble breathing to the point of life-threatening anaphylaxis. Many people who know that they have shellfish allergies carry epinephrine injectors in case of accidental exposure, but not everyone who has a shellfish allergy is aware of it.

A protein called tropomyosin that plays a role in muscle contractions is generally the guilty party when a shellfish allergy strikes. A version of the protein found in vertebrates doesn't provoke allergic responses in humans. But the invertebrate forms of tropomyosin are similar enough to one another that if a person is allergic to one crustacean, they are usually (but not always) allergic to crab, shrimp and lobster alike – and if allergic to one mollusc, to all molluscs. Most food-processing procedures don't weaken tropomyosin, so crab and other shellfish can cause allergic reactions whether they are raw, cooked or pasteurized.

Shellfish poisoning is another problem, and one that is often misdiagnosed as an allergic reaction, since the symptoms are similar – and similarly severe.[15] Algal blooms known as red tides, like the one that struck California coasts in 2015, can contain toxins that contaminate crabs and other sea-life. If eaten, meat from contaminated animals can cause gastrointestinal and neurological symptoms including temporary paralysis, seizures, memory loss and, in the most severe cases, respiratory failure. People who have eaten crab or other shellfish without incident and then suddenly have a reaction are left wondering what is safe to eat in the future. Another disclosure: my partner once had to be rushed from a seafood bar to a hospital emergency room when anaphylactic shock set in after she ate a crab cake, even though she had eaten them many times prior. Allergy tests were inconclusive, so before travelling to two major seafood capitals, her allergist asked her to bring frozen and canned crab to the office for a 'crab challenge': she would eat the stuff that had made her ill with nurses nearby in case she needed treatment. After she passed this formidable test, doctors decided she had suffered a poisoning incident, not

an allergic reaction, and she was free to eat her way through New Orleans and Tokyo without fear of accidental crab exposure.

There are crab-like alternatives, but the imitation crabmeat marketed as seafood sticks, 'krab' or surimi (literally, in Japanese, ground meat) is not a reliable substitute for those who are allergic to shellfish or following religious proscriptions, because minute amounts of crab or lobster extract may be used as flavouring. Japanese cookbooks dating to at least 1528 contain surimi recipes, and the process of making a paste from minced fish is probably much older.[16] Researchers at the entity now known as the Hokkaido National Fisheries Research Institute in the north of Japan developed techniques for processing fish into surimi in commercial quantities in the late 1960s, using mild, lean fishes like pollock or whiting and adding water, starches, non-piscine proteins, sweeteners, preservatives, dyes and flavourings – for example, tapioca or potato, soy or egg whites, sugar or sorbitol, seaweed-based carrageenan, paprika or monosodium glutamate (MSG).

Before large manufacturers industrialized the preparation of surimi, cooks rarely finished it in forms mimicking animal parts, but the Japanese and American companies that teamed up to put surimi in u.s. markets pushed the product as imitation crab or, less often, lobster or scallop. The first large-scale surimi product in the United States was branded 'Sea Legs', and packaged in the form of sticks, tinted to mimic king crab legs.[17] Also packaged in chunks, slivers or flakes, imitation crab is used as filler in shellfish salads, cakes or croquettes, and it is slipped into just about every California roll served in sushi restaurants. Is it crab? Not even close. Is it sustainable, as a cheap alternative to more fragile meats? Not if overfishing continues to decimate oceanic fish stocks. Surimi production hovered at around 800,000 tonnes each year from 2011 to 2018, with prices rising as fisheries in India, China and Vietnam found their catches of silver carp, bream and other tropical fish reduced by extreme weather events, smaller fish size and other factors.[18] Someday, heavily processed, endlessly malleable imitation crab may be nearly as precious as some of the crusty, clawed-animal protein sources it pretends to replace.

Seaweed salad roll with crab stick.

Not all the crab we consume is in the form of foodstuff. For example, the popular over-the-counter dietary supplement glucosamine is mostly made from the shells of crabs, shrimps and lobsters. Labels often warn that it contains a potential allergen, but studies suggest that the shells used in its manufacture don't contain the protein that triggers allergic reactions, and that most people can take glucosamine without concern.[19] The Atlantic horseshoe crab (*Limulus polyphemus*), a chelicerate rather than a crustacean, is also a surprising source of pharmaceutical products.

In 1956, Fred Bang, working at the Marine Biological Laboratory at Woods Hole, showed that the horseshoe crab's blue blood contains cells – the amoebocytes – that coagulate rapidly to isolate introduced bacteria. He developed a way to use their blood to test batches of drugs and other medicinal products for contamination. Beginning in 1977, when the u.s. Food and Drug Administration approved the use of Limulus amebocyte lysate (LAL), manufacturers phased out more costly and time-consuming tests using live rabbits in favour of LAL testing. To produce LAL, horseshoe crabs are harvested from shores along the United States' Eastern Seaboard, from Massachusetts to South Carolina. Some states limit the harvest to protect the species more aggressively than others. At factories on Cape Cod and elsewhere, blood is drawn from the horseshoe crabs, which are then returned to sea. Estimated mortality rates vary widely, and population crashes due at least in part to overharvesting have cascading effects on other species. If you have ever received a vaccination, blood transfusion, antibiotic, insulin or chemotherapy treatment by injection, been hooked up to an intravenous drip or added a pacemaker, stent, prosthesis or interocular lens to your body, you likely have the horseshoe crab to thank for its safety.[20]

Obviously there are large global markets for fresh and processed crab, and even imitative products and non-food derivatives.

How these products get to markets involves easy-to-romanticize seafaring and numbing manual labour. The blue crab industry in the mid-Atlantic coast of the United States provides a compelling portrait of the role of unglamorous, low-wage labour that puts live whole crabs in fish markets and ready-to-eat crabmeat in grocery stores, targeting consumers without easy access to live, fresh crab. Watermen worked these coasts from the colonial period, catching crab, oysters and other seafood, but the industry could only really flourish in the late nineteenth and early twentieth centuries, when new cooling techniques allowed live crab to be shipped successfully on ice in large numbers to urban markets. William Warner's account of crabbing in the Chesapeake Bay, *Beautiful Swimmers* (1976), describes tough, mostly taciturn men going out to sea, returning on good days with boats loaded with sooks and jimmies – female and male crabs – or, on bad days, not loaded with much at all. For most of the history of post-colonial crab fishing in this region, the watermen have mostly been white men, and their wives have pitched in to sort the catch for size and quality, especially during soft-shell ('peeler') season. Working-class and working-poor African American women long performed much of the work of crab picking at the processing plants, often as one seasonal job among many.[21] African American men were more likely to work in sections of the plants where crab was cooked.

Crab picking is tedious, tiresome work. Pickers use a knife to remove the top shell. They then remove the gills, eyes, legs and stomach, before gently digging 'backfin', 'lump' and 'flake' meat out of the body and extracting claw meat. Since processing plants pay workers according to how many pounds are picked, the work is fast-paced and it requires care and dexterity to dismantle a crab and remove the meat without leaving in shards of shell. Employment depends on the availability of crab to pick, so demand for workers can vary from day to day. Days off due to foul weather or a moratorium on fishing when water quality is poor result in a lower pay cheque, or none at all.

In the late 1980s, the U.S. government initiated a 'guest worker' programme allowing temporary foreign workers to obtain visas to work in specified industries. Companies could apply for these H-2B visas for their desired number of workers. Applications were approved on a first-come, first-serve basis, until the federal cap on this type of visa was reached. Women from Mexico began to displace local workers in the Chesapeake Bay area, some of whom chose to pursue growing opportunities in education, tourism and health care in the area; others felt pushed out of their jobs.[22] Federal law allows employers to pay non-agricultural guest workers less than the minimum wage, making H-2B workers cheaper to hire than locals. In many communities they became key members of the labour force. As recently as 2017, plants in Hoopers Island, Maryland, employed some six hundred guest workers arriving annually for seasonal stints.[23]

The following year, when the federal government made changes to the guest worker programme, four plants on Hoopers Island shut down for lack of workers. Economists have estimated that hiring one guest worker ensures the stability of two-and-a-half other local jobs, from crab fishing and bait sales to trucking and icemakers; processors forced to sell whole instead of picked crabs when labor is in short supply can expect far less per pound.[24] In other words, it is not only environmental conditions that can punch economic holes in crabbing communities. Political turmoil around immigration issues can also destabilize industries and the small communities in which they operate.[25]

Still, conditions for H-2B workers can be arduous, given the unpredictable availability of work, low wages and rules forbidding workers from quitting to work for another employer in the same industry.[26] Studies of these workers have revealed problems with lax health and safety provisions, wage theft and illegal fees, and overcrowded or substandard housing, which workers typically rent from their employers close to processing plants but isolated from public transportation or towns for grocery shopping.[27] Simple cuts, which are common workplace injuries, put these women at risk of the dangerous bacterial infection *Vibrio vulnificus*.

Mid-Atlantic crab pickers aren't the only ones facing work-related health issues. 'Crab asthma' results when workers become sensitive to allergens aerosolized when crabs are cut up and cooked. A study published in 2003 showed that 18 per cent of workers in four plants processing snow crab in the Canadian provinces of Newfoundland and Labrador 'had certain or highly probable crab asthma'. Prevalence depended on how well ventilated each plant was, as well as differences in processing methods.[28] Nearly a decade later, another team of researchers found even higher rates of symptoms typical of occupational asthma: 45 per cent in a study of snow crab workers, most of them Inuit, in Greenland – even if these cases were vastly underreported.[29]

Workers in crab processing plants labour under conditions that can be precarious, physically taxing, repetitive, poorly compensated and little understood. In contrast, off North America's northwestern coasts, crab-fishing crews have been lionized in the Discovery Channel's reality television series *The Deadliest Catch*. At the time of writing, the show is in its fifteenth season; its pilot aired in 2004 and subsequent seasons contained between ten and nineteen episodes. That's a lot of crab TV. Reality TV producer Thom Beers, founder of Original Productions, put film crews aboard several vessels sailing out of Dutch Harbor, Alaska, capturing the fierce competition to locate crab, collect full pots – which are actually heavy steel and nylon cages up to 3 m (10 ft) in length – and get them to shore quickly. Commercial fishing has long ranked as one of the most dangerous professions in the United States, with only logging sometimes leading to more fatalities per year.[30] Conditions in the Bering Sea make work there especially hazardous. It's risky business, conducted in freezing temperatures, driving rain and rolling seas. The big catches are Alaskan or red king crab (*Paralithodes camtschaticus*), as well as members of the Chionoectes genus known as snow crab, queen crab, opilio crab ('opies') and bairdi, or tanner, crab.

The Deadliest Catch turns hard physical labour into a genre that is part soap opera, part action adventure. 'Greenhorns' try their hand at the job for the first time, with lots of blood, sweat and tears. Old rivals squabble over territory and technique. Injuries abound, in the form of crushed fingers, swollen hands, jellyfish stings. Heavy equipment, sharp tools and 7 to 12 m (25 to 40 ft) waves create obstacle courses. Sometimes death-defying risks pay off, and the money shot is crabs – huge, hard, long-legged, wriggling crabs – pouring out of pots to be sorted by hand, with females and male 'smalls' that don't meet minimum legal size

The Deadliest Catch: a crew hauls in a crab pot.

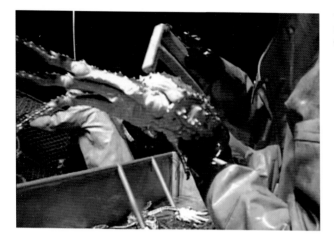

The Deadliest Catch: measuring crabs.

tossed back. (King crabs must have at least 178-mm-wide (7 in.) carapaces; tanner crabs 140 mm (5.5 in.).)[31] Catches are described in hundreds of thousands of dollars, not the dollars and cents per pound paid to u.s. East Coast pickers. In one episode an off-screen narrator describes a crew that 'scoops up crab in a lucrative money pit'. Full pots of crab are a jackpot, a 'modern day gold rush', 'going platinum'.

But the show isn't just about fighting the elements for not-so-easy money, and most workers don't get the biggest slice of the profits. The show promises real-life tragedy, and it delivers. To start the show's first season, the narrator announced: 'On average, the Bering sea will claim the life of one unlucky soul every week of the season . . . Over the next two crab seasons, men will die.' The men know it, too; their families gather to pray together before they ship out, 'maybe for the last time'. A few episodes later, five crew members aboard the *Big Valley* died when it capsized, and one drowned after falling overboard from the *Sultan*. When Captain Phil Harris of the *Cornelia Marie* died of a stroke in season six, his sons carried on, their grief part of the narrative. The youngest, Jake, once a greenhorn, becomes a captain himself. Risking everything and shouldering the burden of carrying on familial traditions, these men's ruggedness is more glamourized than lesser-known labours in the industry. Theirs is an arduous form of resource extracting, hauling crab out of stormy seas for shipping to faraway markets, where consumers queue up for sweet, messy, pricey crab legs.

Not only are there people who love crabmeat so much that they will organize holidays around seasonal catches or spar over the last serving of crab on a smorgasbord; there are also people who love crabmeat enough that they will watch other people eat it. Not just crab, however; in the streaming-video genre known as mukbang (a portmanteau of the Korean words for 'eat' and 'broadcast') that originated in South Korea in about 2009, on-screen eaters consume large portions of all kinds of foods for millions of viewers. One of the practice's successful performer-eaters is a seafood-boil specialist. Bethany Gaskin of Cincinnati, Ohio, first ventured onto YouTube in 2017 with cooking demonstrations, but soon tried a mukbang video under the name Bloveslife, and her social media career took off. In one of her most popular videos, Bethany eats a 4-kilogram (9 lb) king crab that she calls Curtis Senior, having eaten a somewhat smaller crab she called Curtis Junior in another video. The huge dead crab sits on a table with a bowl of her signature sauce to the side. Bethany tears the legs off, pulling out the meat, dipping it in sauce and taking huge bites. The sound of shell cracking competes with her lip-smacking and murmurs of pleasure. Her blouse's puffed sleeves, long painted nails and multiple pieces of jewellery don't seem to suffer even as sauce drips down her chin and coats her fingers. She namechecks the supplier and claims that the crab cost $500 – 'definitely worth it'. She occasionally refers to the meal as 'lobster', and at one point is confused about whether the crab came from Alaska or Australia, but she praises the quality of the meat. When she finishes the legs she digs into the shell, then moves on to the claws. The video lasts 44 minutes, interrupted frequently by paid advertising, a boon to both YouTube and Gaskin herself: she's earned over a million dollars since starting mukbang. The eating isn't really eroticized, and the video itself is run of the mill, with a static camera, out-of-the-box editing effects and a garish aquarium background. Whether viewers watch for a vicarious brush with a food they can't afford or otherwise can't eat, or whether they watch for gross-out laughs, is a bit of a mystery, at least to this writer.

But they do watch. Bloveslife's Curtis Senior video has had some 2.2 million views at the time of writing, and her YouTube channels have almost as many subscribers.[32] She isn't even the most popular mukbang star. Another eater named Min Ga-in, who posts as Dorothy, uploaded a king crab mukbang to YouTube late in 2018, which has already gained over 17 million views. She speaks in Korean, almost whispering, and the video is subtitled in English. She's not as chatty as Gaskin, but pants between bites and chews loudly. She moves at a faster pace, clocking in at sixteen minutes, opting for fast-motion segments while she clears away gills and other inedible parts, but she is determined to finish. Coaxing meat out of the knuckles, she chides her meal: 'Come out, come out or I will get mad.' After showing off the empty shell and taking a long drink of chamomile tea, she declares: 'Enjoyed eating a lot. This was [a] very meaningful battle.'[33]

Many but not all mukbang eaters are women. Mukbang poster Kaneko wanted so badly to eat the biggest crab he could find that he travelled from Japan to Tasmania to eat a Tasmanian king crab (*Pseudocarcinus gigas*), which he filmed being boiled alive and eaten at a seafood warehouse. The claw alone is as long as his forearm. In Bloveslife and Dorothy's posts, the cameras are trained

Charlotte Seid,
*Armed Box
Crab (Playmera
gaudichaudii)*,
2019, ink on paper.

steadily on their eating, but Kaneko's camera roams the warehouse, and only a fraction of his fifteen-minute video shows him eating. He doesn't even finish the crab, taking one claw back to his hotel room. But then, the crab weighed some 10 kg (22 lb) and cost 170,000 yen (which the video title equates to $1,500), plus travel expenses. One of over 6,000 comments made in response to Kaneko's video suggests an ambivalent viewer: 'i eat a lot of crabs. but this one i feel like i want to keep it live longer.'[34]

Too late. Kaneko, like fellow mukbang videomakers Bloveslife and Dorothy, has vanquished the crab. As have crab fishermen on coasts all over the world, for centuries, and as have eager eaters on buffet queues, at crab festivals, seafood restaurants and seaside shacks. We have loved crabmeat so much that we have made minor celebrities not only of some of the captains and crews that fish for crabs, but of a few social media stars willing to gorge themselves on camera. In reality – even more so than reality TV – bringing crab to market is hard work, hazardous and, for most workers, undercompensated. That work is widely unrecognized when we take up our crab mallets and seafood forks, and when it is recognized it is often the most daring of the lot who capture our attention: those whose lives are on the line during fishing season. Fortunately, while commercial fishing remains one of the most hazardous occupations, in recent years crab fishing has become much safer. From the 1980s to the early 2000s, the average number of deaths associated with crab fishing in the United States dropped from 37 to 11 per year. During most of the early twenty-first century, U.S. East Coast cod, flounder and scallop fishing accidents have resulted in more deaths than Bering Sea crabbing.[35] Even one workplace death is too many, to be sure. But almost no one mourns the crab.

6 A World Without Crabs

What is this little guy's job in the world. If this little
guy dies does the world know? Does the world feel this?
Does something get displaced? If this little guy dies does
the world get a little lighter? Does the planet rotate a
little faster? If this little guy dies, without his body to shift
the currents of air, does the air flow perceptibly faster?
What shifts if this little guy dies? Do people speak language
a little bit differently? If this little guy dies does some little
kid somewhere wake up with a bad dream? Does an
almost imperceptible link in the chain snap? Will
civilization stumble?
David Wojnarowicz (1990)[1]

One of the defining characteristics of the human-animal relationship is how we are making animals' habitats (and our own)
unbearable: ever more shrunken, fragmented, acidified and hot.
What happens when our socio-economic activities disrupt their
livelihoods? As humans, as we go about our daily lives we eat
animals and use animal products, burn fossil fuels, deforest vast
acreage and pollute the world's waters with chemicals and
plastics. In doing so, how are we affecting the capacity of non-
human animals to go about their daily lives?

This chapter considers our relationships to crabs that are
experiencing the acute effects of anthropogenic climate change,
human-produced pollutants, habitat destruction and resource
extraction. These conditions are, in no small measure, components of the history we have shared with these animals. And
they are signs of the ways in which, even though animals including the crab play roles in our mythologies, our arts, our cuisines
and our labours, we have failed to consider their needs in our
future-making.

While many crab populations are robust, the status of many others is unknown. Consider how many species have only been recently discovered. Their distribution, especially on the barely explored ocean floor, is yet to be fully understood. Some are endangered, threatened or vulnerable. The habitats of many crabs are in trouble. For example, scientists can map increasing ocean acidification – that is, falling pH levels as a result of increasing carbon dioxide – over the course of the past two centuries, showing the impact of Industrial Age practices. Average pH levels in the world's seas has dropped from 8.2 to 8.1 over this period. While this may not sound like much, the scale is logarithmic: a decrease of 0.1 constitutes a 30 per cent increase in acidity.

The Bering Sea, which is subject to volatile seasonal changes, is most acidic during the winter months, when pH levels can drop as low as 7.7.[2] Increasing acidity may eventually reduce king and snow crab populations, including the commercially fished red, blue, tanner, bairdi and opilio crabs. Different species may

Blueberry Hermit Crab (Coenobita purpureus) in Plastic Cap, 2015. The cap fits a cassette gas tank, such as those used with portable gas stoves. The caps are often discarded on beaches, like this one in Okinawa, Japan.

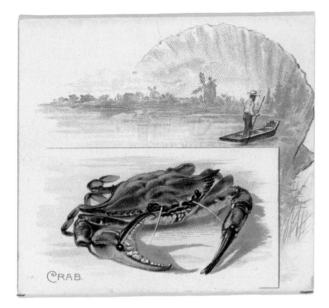

A trading card in the 'Fish from American Water' series promoting Allen & Ginter cigarettes, 1889.

respond differently to changing conditions, but acidic waters seem to make it more taxing for these animals to produce shells, slowing growth rates and increasing mortality during moults, especially in juvenile stages.[3] It remains to be seen if these crabs can adapt quickly enough to survive in changing seas.

We don't see many of the animals that are affected by our human actions – the ones that lose their homes when we drain wetlands, for example. We do, however, notice when the economically important ones go missing. As oceanic low-oxygen (hypoxic) dead zones have proliferated, widespread populations of ocean life have crashed. Among them, the Chesapeake Bay blue crab, which has dramatically diminished in number several times. Overfishing is a factor, but so is pollution. When nitrogen and phosphorus in agricultural run-off and urban waste streams make their way into the ocean, they also feed the growth of algae that choke off sea grasses that young crabs need to hide in. The algae also smother other forms of life, leaving sea creatures of all kinds struggling to breathe in the oxygen-depleted water. Too many die to reproduce a robust next generation. In the case of Western Atlantic blue crabs, that means a loss of jobs in fishing, processing and other related forms of employment.[4] Fortunately, for blue crabs and for those who make their living from them, restoration projects put in place by federal and state governments have reduced run-off, reviving moribund sea grass beds and making progress towards cleaning up habitats for not only the blue crab but for oysters and other creatures.[5]

Long-term low oxygen events can deplete animal populations and the human industries that exploit them. We should understand them as signs of sick seas. But some short-term low oxygen events have long been celebrated as harbingers of good fortune and the ocean's abundance. Conditions in Mobile Bay, Alabama, result in hypoxic events several times each summer, when the tide is weak, the air is still, and fresh water and salt water don't mix, depriving the deepest waters of oxygen. Shrimp, flounder and other bottom-dwelling fish seek more oxygenated water in the shallows and may wash ashore. Crabs, which can breathe out of water so long as their gills remain wet, may actually crawl out of the sea and into the hands and nets of seafood-loving humans. This phenomenon is known as 'jubilee', in which animals just trying to breathe become easy pickings for impromptu feasts. Mobile Bay was once the only place where jubilees were known to occur regularly. Now, a combination of natural conditions, severe weather and the accumulation of nitrogen-rich pollution is making them occur more frequently and in unexpected places along the u.s. shores of the Gulf of Mexico.[6] Jubilees might sound festive, but the conditions that produce them are funereal.

Previously, I described the charming habits of male banana fiddler crabs, *Uca mjoebergi*, who wave their biggest claw in hopes of attracting mates. How is climate change impacting these little crabs in Australia's Darwin Harbour? Scientific consensus says that fossil fuel emissions and widespread deforestation have worked hand-in-hand with global warming to increase gases, including carbon dioxide (CO_2), in the Earth's atmosphere. The result is global warming, with the planet's averages increasing 0.85°C between 1880 and 2012, and continuing to rise with alarming consequences.[7] Global warming produces higher atmospheric temperatures and rising seas, in part because water expands as it warms, and because glaciers and other large bodies of ice are melting into the seas. Rises in temperature and sea level affect *U. mjoebergi*, the banana fiddler.[8] Sea-level rise has already reduced the amount of suitable habitat, pressing *U. mjoebergi* and *U. elegans*, a Northern Territory fiddler that prefers salt flats, into overlapping territory, with as yet uncertain outcome. Less obviously, rising temperatures impact the crabs' reproductive cycles.

Female banana fiddler crabs choose when to mate and whom to mate with by selecting the male with the largest claw or fastest

Male banana fiddler crabs (*Uca mjoebergi*) sparring.

wave, or the one who waves before other males. They also engage in these activities on a schedule. Upon choosing a potential mate, a female inspects his burrow. If it is to her liking she settles down while he seals the burrow entrance with sand. He deposits his sperm, which she stores for up to five days while he guards her. Once she expels the eggs, allowing them to come into contact with the stored sperm, the male leaves, closing up the burrow again and going off to find a new burrow for himself. The female stays put while the eggs incubate. She stays underground until the eggs mature into larvae capable of fending for themselves. This stage takes about sixteen days and must be timed precisely. Females must mate, tend to fertilization of the eggs and allow them to mature just in time for the highest tide of the month, which unplugs the burrow and washes the larval crabs to sea. Eventually, they return to shore, in the form of juvenile crabs.

Under warmer conditions – say, if the female incubates her eggs in a burrow that gets full sun rather than lots of shade – the eggs mature a little faster. The female can adjust the period between mating and fertilization somewhat, so that the eggs are ready for release when that big high tide rolls in. But this stage of reproduction is not endlessly flexible. If the eggs mature before high tide, they'll languish in the burrow and never make it out to sea. As temperatures rise, the timing of each reproductive cycle becomes more precarious and the chance of diminishing numbers of viable offspring increases.[9]

Why would it matter if populations of this small, short-lived crab plummeted? Banana fiddlers may seem quite preoccupied with their own mating games and territorial spats, but in fact they play key roles in the mangrove forests that are their natural habitat, so much so that some researchers refer to them as 'ecosystem engineers'.[10] Their burrowing and foraging, even their skittering about, helps keep the sediment layers clean and aerated. They are, unwittingly, working the soils of the estuaries and their banks, controlling bacterial levels, managing the growth of algae and processing decomposing plant material. Undercut these functions? The result is poorer water quality in the estuary that supports the mangroves. Mangrove forests provide habitats for nesting birds and juvenile fish of many oceanic species; they control erosion and trap CO_2. The loss of mangrove forests damages nearby sea grass beds and coral reefs and increases the impact of storms on inlands left unprotected when the trees are destroyed. There are many reasons why tropical mangroves disappear: logging, for one; development for agriculture, aquaculture, shipping or other human uses, for another. With increased warming, crashing crab populations – the decline of the mangroves' own little groundkeepers – may be another.

In habitats such as the mangrove forests, one significant change can have cascading effects throughout flora and fauna, throwing relationships among species out of whack. Changes of this kind include the loss or introduction of predators, loss of food sources, sea-level rise, ocean acidification and deoxygenation, to name a few that can be traced back to human activity. When a species of plant or animal with a particular job to do in an ecosystem – for example, it feeds or is fed upon by other creatures, aerates the soil, cleans up waste, pollinates plants or scatters seeds in its excrement – crashes or proliferates wildly, relationships among many life forms may go awry.

Cape Cod provides another case study of this kind of precarious balance. A peninsula jutting off the U.S. mainland state of Massachusetts into the Atlantic Ocean, the Cape takes the shape of a human arm, bent at the elbow, fist curled inwards. The protected lands of Cape Cod National Seashore contain salt marshes that hold back erosion, soften the blows of big storms and provide habitat for many plants and animals. Some of them are crabs.

I visited one of these marshes with Steve Smith, a plant biologist with the National Park Service, to learn more about them. Meeting in a rutted dirt parking lot at Great Island, in the town of Wellfleet, we both changed into knee-high waders. It was a good thing, too. Steve forged ahead as if comfortable on any terrain while I struggled to keep up in the gluey mud.

Everywhere we looked, fiddler crabs (*Uca pugnax*) skittered away from us, sometimes disappearing entirely into their holes, sometimes peeking out, awaiting their next opportunity to get back above ground. I knew that the males use their major claw to spar with rivals and attract mates. I wondered whether the larger males, positioned half out of their burrows and waving their claws, were trying to scare us off. However charming the fiddlers, and however abundant, they weren't really what we were looking for. Instead, Steve hoped to show me an example of the purple marsh crab (*Sesarma reticulatum*), who is blamed for the bare spots in the marsh that have been cropping up since at least the 1980s.[11] It was mid-morning and the *Sesarma* crab is mostly nocturnal, but eventually Steve spotted one. He plunged his hand into the mud, hoping to catch the crab, but was only nipped. The next time he was luckier and avoided getting pinched as he picked up a gorgeous specimen. While the fiddlers have a thin, flattish carapace, *Sesarma* is boxy. Its body is brown and its limbs glisten purple. Its chelipeds terminate with substantial tawny pincers, and its eyes glare out from relatively short stalks. After a moment, he placed the animal back in the mud to go about its business.

Much of the marsh is green with smooth cord grass (*Spartina alterniflora*), the purple marsh crab's favourite meal. They also eat salt marsh hay (*S. patens*), but they don't like the pickleweed, sea lavender and other non-grassy vegetation that grow in the area.[12] In a more balanced ecosystem, there would be too few of the

Purple marsh crab (*Sesarma reticulatum*) at Great Island, Wellfleet, Massachusetts.

purple marsh crabs to eat more than their fair share. But their numbers have boomed as populations of their predators, including the smooth dogfish, blue crabs and the popular striped bass, have receded with overfishing. The result is salt marsh dieback, marked by bald muddy patches.

Ironically, these grassless mudflats are unsuitable for deep, intricate *S. reticulatum* burrows, but *U. pugnax* is happy to make its more shallow, shorter tunnels in the denuded mud. So the fiddler population density increases, too, leading to more burrowing and foraging on the mudflats. In Cape Cod's dieback areas, researchers counted an average of 134 fiddler burrows per square metre, a good amount more than in other areas where they live along the Western Atlantic coast.[13] Even though the fiddlers themselves don't eat the cord grass, where they are this abundant their numerous burrows and their constant sifting of the peat makes it even more difficult for grass seedlings to take root where they could fill the bare patches back in.[14]

Salt marsh die-off is easily traced to the loss of purple marsh crab predators, which has allowed the crab to become so numerous that it is damaging its own habitat. What would we lose if the marshes continue to die back? What is the marsh's job, so to speak? Like mangrove forests, salt marshes are home to nesting birds and stopover sites for migrating birds and butterflies. They are breeding grounds for oceanic fish. They protect inlands from storm surges. And they absorb and store massive amounts of carbon dioxide. Marsh dieback undercuts the role of these important ecosystems in slowing the rate of climate change, increases our vulnerability to severe weather events, and depletes resources for a far-reaching array of animal life.[15] Strangely enough, an invasive species may help restore these habitats. European green crabs adapt readily to new environments. They don't dig their own burrows but will take over *Sesarma* burrows, reducing purple marsh crab density, which gives the cord grass a chance of recovering.

The purple marsh crab and mud fiddlers aren't the only crabs on Cape Cod, even if they are some of the most prominent brachyurans – the 'true' crabs – along this part of the Western Atlantic Ocean. Perhaps the most recognized crab of all on these shores is not a crab at all: the Atlantic or American horseshoe crab, *Limulus polyphemus*. To most of us who encounter horseshoe crabs on sandy beaches, their hard shells and ten legs appear pretty crab-like. In fact, they are chelicerates, more closely related to spiders and scorpions than to crustaceans, even if their lifestyles and ecological niches are quite similar to those of many true crabs and anomurans.[16] In the nineteenth century, and the first half of the twentieth century, millions of horseshoe crab – an estimated 1 to 5 million per year – were harvested for fertilizer, livestock feed and bait to be used in other fisheries.[17] Sometimes, shellfishermen did away with horseshoe crabs they saw as competition for clams. Populations dropped so low that the commercial harvesting stalled for a time, then began ticking upwards in the 1970s, with horseshoe crabs again being used as bait in conch, eel and other fisheries. Even now, some horseshoe crabs get caught up in dredging or trawling operations, and it is not known how many are killed in the process. And the medical industry uses the horseshoe crab in huge numbers.

I have described how pharmaceutical companies have, for several decades, used a product made from horseshoe crab blood to detect endotoxins in medical devices, vaccines and other drugs. Hundreds of thousands of horseshoe crabs are harvested, bled and returned to sea annually by a handful of companies specializing in this process, while conservationists express concern that the mortality rate is unacceptable. Millions of shorebirds – especially the red knot – rely on horseshoe crab eggs as a food source. When the eggs are sparse, the bird population declines, too. With robust new commercial users hungry for large numbers of these animals, and with increasing evidence of the importance of horseshoe crabs to other species, in 1998 the Atlantic States Marine Fisheries Commission began to oversee and regulate the harvests. The largest catches are taken from Delaware Bay (Maryland, Virginia, Delaware, New Jersey), with active harvests also concentrated in New York, Massachusetts, and to a lesser extent, elsewhere along the u.s. Eastern Seaboard. The regulation includes annual surveys conducted wherever the horseshoe crabs live and breed, in a vast collaboration between university-based researchers, governmental agencies, non-governmental organizations and volunteers. I joined two survey teams in 2018.

On a grey and blustery May morning, I arrived at Indian Neck Beach in Wellfleet, Massachusetts. The beach occupies a piece of land that is shaped like a crab's left claw, curving towards the mainland to form the inlet known as Chipman's Cove. Just before high tide, members of our team began to arrive. Janet, a retired nurse and volunteer for the Wellfleet Bay Wildlife Sanctuary, led the team and doled out the equipment we used to survey the horseshoe crab population in a section of this beach, including a clipboard with forms for recording today's data.

Janet planted one pole in the ground at the furthest reach of high tide, and I planted another pole 10 m (32 ft) down the shore, pulling the rope that connects these two poles taut. Another volunteer, wearing shorts and sneakers, strode into the chilly bay to hold the third pole out in the bay, so that we formed a square with three sides defined by the ropes. The fourth team member, a college student studying wildlife conservation, waded in to scan for spawning horseshoe crabs, calling out to a volunteer on shore what she saw before we moved our poles down the beach. In each patch we covered, the count was zero. We found five or six dead females on shore. All but one seemed to have died within hours. Their shells were still damp and they had not yet been scavenged by seagulls. Janet said that these 'ladies' would have been trying to lay eggs, and just didn't make it back into the water in time.

The turbidity of the water could have been a factor in our null count. With such brisk winds and choppy waters, there could have been crabs that we couldn't see not far offshore, or they might have found the water too churned up to dare a trip to the beach. And horseshoe crabs could have been harvested from this beach the previous night.

A few days later, on the evening of a full moon late in May, I joined another horseshoe crab survey, this one on a beach in Staten Island's Great Kills, which is part of the Gateway National Recreation Area. Halting rush-hour traffic and twisting residential streets eventually gave way to an expanse of land facing the Atlantic Ocean, much vaster and wilder than I had anticipated. Kathy, an educator for the National Park Service, and her son,

José, a graduate student in biology, led a group of twenty or so spectators, mostly parents with young children, along a bumpy road to a spot called Crooke's Point, where a dozen men were fishing even as the sun set. Taking a few steps into the water, Kathy addressed the group while male horseshoe crabs investigated her boots, brown and round-toed, which they seem to have mistaken for female crabs. Their eager confusion was good for a few laughs. She picked one up and showed us how to tell males from females: females are generally larger and their first pair of legs terminate with pincers; the smaller males have blunt claspers, shaped like boxing gloves, that they use to latch onto females during mating.

Volunteering to help with the survey, I was given a pen and clipboard with a simple form attached. I was told to make a tick mark whenever José called out that he spotted mating horseshoe crabs, indicating whether they were males or females and whether they were fully submerged or exposed in the shallower surf. José and I both had on tall rubber boots, and he waded in. I followed and scrambled to keep up. He began: 'One female, two

Horseshoe crabs
mating, Great Kills,
Staten Island,
New York.

Tagging a horseshoe crab for tracking via www.fws.gov/crabtag.

males submerged. Two females, four males, surf. Three males, submerged. One female, submerged. One female, three males, submerged . . . Four females, eight – no, nine males, surf.' I made marks as fast as I could, occasionally distracted by the sheer quantities of these animals and by a spectacular orange moon-rise. A flock of plovers was usually in sight 18 m (20 yards) or so ahead of us on the beach, going for freshly laid eggs. My form was filling up, and I resorted to the margins and smaller ticks to keep up. After thirty or forty minutes of counting we arrived at a long jetty made of large rocks. The kids in the group gathered around and helped me count up the tick marks. We counted over 650 crabs, all engaged in spawning activity.

Horseshoe crab with beach roses tattoo.

Why were the results of this survey on Staten Island so different from those on the survey I accompanied on Cape Cod? For one thing, I was at Great Kills on the night of a full moon, which seems to be the crabs' favourite time to spawn, although one would expect some activity a few days before and after as well. Weather conditions matter, too; on the day of the survey at Indian Neck, gusty winds made for less than ideal conditions. The role of each state in managing its horseshoe crab population also plays an important role. Where the fishing and biomedical industries are allowed to take higher numbers of crabs, their population may be more vulnerable. Where the harvests are more limited, these animals, which do not reach sexual maturity until around ten years of age, have more opportunities to mate and reproduce.[18]

What would shift in the Western Atlantic ecosystem if the horseshoe crab population plummeted again? We could expect unhealthier seas and shores, for one thing. Their skittering movements may help aerate seabed floors, making it easier for oysters and clams to thrive. Horseshoe crabs are a vital food source for sea turtles, as well as shorebirds, some of them long-distance migrators. Many of those birds also eat worms, beetles, weevils, flies, snails, moths and other creatures that, unless controlled by predators, can do significant damage to fruit, rice, cotton and other crops. Clearly, the ebbs and flows of the horseshoe crab population, influenced by anthropogenic activity, have cascading effects on other animals, and on our own food security.

But the price of corn shouldn't be the primary determinant of whether or not the horseshoe crab, or any other animal, deserves protection from profit-driven industries and their malignant externalities: hazardous waste, habitat destruction, greenhouse gases, excessive exploitation. Ancestors of modern horseshoe crabs have been found in fossils dating back as far as 485 MYA, and they are remarkably similar to the surviving members of the genera *Limulidae*. Horseshoe crabs, like their distant cousins the true crabs and anomurans, are fascinating creatures that don't need us to live their lives: they've been doing so, with remarkable success, for hundreds of millions of years before our own species, *Homo sapiens*, evolved. Time will tell if they will continue to do so in spite of human appetites and wastefulness.

Does 'the world get a little lighter? Does the planet rotate a little faster?', if anthropogenic activities change the climate, warming, acidifying and deoxygenating of our oceans? We know that king and snow crabs in the Bering Sea are vulnerable to these changes. We may notice their decline first as the price of these delicacies at seafood markets and restaurants rises. But we are not the only species in the food chain that would miss them. Bearded seals, halibut, cod, octopi and otters would also suffer from a reduction in the crabs' numbers. Likewise, higher atmospheric temperatures and sea-level rise on Australia's Northern

Horseshoe crabs and plastic pollution, Great Kills, Staten Island, New York.

Territory is testing the banana fiddlers that live around Darwin Harbour, threatening to incubate some of their eggs too quickly for them to be washed out to sea at high tide. In this eventuality, future generations of the crab may not be numerous enough to do their jobs tidying up the mangrove forests in which they live. The mangroves, like the salt marshes of the u.s. Eastern Seaboard, define the coasts and are home to countless species. While the salt marshes may be vulnerable to over-grazing by too-abundant marsh crabs, it's equally true that those crabs, and the mud fiddlers with whom they share the marshes, are integral to the ecosystem. A world without crabs would be a vastly impoverished, even impossible world.

Timeline of the Crab

(Lower Ordovician-Silurian) Ancient kin of modern horseshoe crabs inhabit what are now Manitoba, Morocco and southern England

c. 259 MYA

(Upper Permian) Anomura and Brachyura clades diverge

c. 400 BCE

The Greek physician Hippocrates refers to certain kinds of tumours as *karkinos*, likening their shape to that of a crab

c. 350 BCE

In his *History of Animals*, Aristotle declares: 'Of the crab, the varieties are indefinite and incalculable'

1886

Mary J. Rathbun goes to work at the Smithsonian Institution; she goes on to describe 1,147 crab species before her death in 1943

c. 1887–9

Dutch painter Vincent van Gogh completes two paintings of crabs: *A Crab on Its Back*, now at the Van Gogh Museum in Amsterdam, and *Two Crabs*, now at the National Gallery in London

1957

Roger Corman's low-budget monster movie *Attack of the Crab Monsters* pits giant mutating land crabs against scientists studying the aftermath of nuclear weapons testing on Bikini Atoll

---

1989

Disney's *The Little Mermaid* introduces Sebastian the Crab, sidekick to King Triton, minder of the king's daughter Ariel, and musician

1999

Nickelodeon launches the series *SpongeBob SquarePants*, whose characters include the cantankerous Mr Krabs, owner of the Krusty Krab restaurant

2000

The Census of Marine Life begins, supporting deep-sea research that leads to the discovery of thousands of new species, including the 'yeti' crab

2004

The Discovery Channel airs the pilot for *The Deadliest Catch*, a long-running reality TV series tracking the action aboard crab fishing vessels in the Bering Sea

1185	c. 1817	c. 1870s	1872–6

Heike warriors die at sea in the Battle of Dan-no-ura in the Sea of Japan, inspiring a myth that they are reincarnated as Heike-gani crabs, whose backs uncannily resemble a scowling face

The invasive European green or shore crab, *Carcinus maenas*, is first observed in the Western Atlantic, on coastal Massachusetts

James McMenamin establishes the first factory to successfully can crab, in Hampton, Virginia

The HMS *Challenger* sails the world's seas, while researchers aboard collect specimens, including the first described 'blanket-hermit' crab

c. 1960s	1976	1977	1977

The Hokkaido National Fisheries Research Institute in Japan develops a technique for processing fish and other ingredients into a form of surimi that mimics crabmeat

James Michener's epic novel *Chesapeake* features a short-lived character named Jimmy, a blue crab that doesn't survive the polluting flood that ravaged the Chesapeake Bay in 1886

The U.S. Food and Drug Administration approves the use of LAL, a derivative of horseshoe crab blood, to detect harmful bacteria in pharmaceutical products

Beautiful Swimmers: Watermen, Crabs and the Chesapeake Bay by William W. Warner wins the Pulitzer Prize in General Nonfiction

2005	2017	2018

Javier Luque finds an unusual fossil in Colombia different from any other known brachyuran or anomuran. *Callichimaera perplexa* becomes an Internet sensation when his description is first published in 2019

Members of the Kani tribe in the Western Ghat mountains of India show a team of researchers a fully arboreal crab, which they name *Kani maranjandun*

Several crab-processing plants on Hoopers Island, Maryland, close when changes in the guest worker visa programme allow for too few seasonal workers

References

1 WHAT IS A CRAB?

1 Previous generations of scientists lumped together lobsters, shrimps and prawns in the group Macrura ('long tailed') but more modern classification systems treat them separately. See Rev. Thomas R. R. Stebbing, *A History of Crustacea: Recent Malacostraca* (London, 1893).

2 Patsy A. McLaughlin and Talbot Murray, '*Clibanarius fonticola*, New Species (Anomura: Paguridea: Diogenidea), from a Freshwater Pool on Espiritu Santo, Vanuatu', *Journal of Crustacean Biology*, x/4 (1990), pp. 695–702.

3 More detailed information on bromeliad crabs and other aspects of crab life cycles is found in Judith S. Weis, *Walking Sideways: The Remarkable World of Crabs* (Ithaca, NY, 2012), pp. 62–84.

4 Jean Genet, *Funeral Rites*, trans. Bernard Frechtman (New York, 1970), pp. 41–2; first published as *Pompes funebres* (Paris, 1953).

5 Dave Rudkin, Graham Young and Godfrey Nowlan, 'The Oldest Horseshoe Crab: A New Xiphosurid from Late Ordovician Konservat-Lagerstätten Deposits, Manitoba, Canada', *Palaeontology*, LI/1 (2008), pp. 1–9.

6 Derek E. G. Briggs et al., 'Silurian Horseshoe Crab Illuminates the Evolution of Arthropod Limbs', *PNAS*, CIX/39 (2012), pp. 15,702–5.

7 Peter Van Roy, Derek E. G. Briggs and Robert R. Gaines, 'The Fezouata Fossils of Morocco: An Extraordinary Record of Marine Life in the Early Ordovician', *Journal of the Geological Society*, CLXXII (2015), pp. 541–9.

8 See Thomas Huxley, *Geological Contemporaneity and Persistent Types of Life: The Anniversary Address to the Geological Society for 1862*, ebook, www.gutenberg.org.

9 Adrian Kin and Błażej Błażejowski, 'The Horseshoe Crab of the Genus *Limulus*: Living Fossil or Stabilomorph?', *PLOS ONE*, IX/10 (2014). The authors define 'stabilomorphs' as creatures minimally changed over 65 million or more years, and survivors of at least one mass extinction event.

10 Heather Bracken-Grissom et al., 'A Comprehensive and Integrative Reconstruction of Evolutionary History for Anomura (Crustacea: Decapoda)', *BMC Evolutionary Biology*, XIII/128 (2013).

11 Jérôme Chablais, Rodney M. Feldmann and Carrie E. Schweitzer, 'A New Triassic Decapod, *Plattykotta akaina*, from the Arabian Shelf of the Northern United Arab Emirates: Earliest Occurrence of the Anomura', *Paläontologishe Zeitschrift*, XXCV (2011), pp. 93–102.

12 L. A. Borradaile, 'Crustacea Part II Porcellanopagurus: An Instance of Carcinerisation', British Antarctic ('Terra Nova') Expedition, 1910, Natural History Report, *Zoology*, III/3 (1916), pp. 111–26.

13 Carrie E. Schweitzer and Rodney M. Feldman, 'The Oldest Brachyura (Decapoda: Homolodromomioidea: Glaessneropsidea) Known to Date (Jurassic)', *Journal of Crustacean Biology*, XXX/2 (2010), pp. 251–6.

14 See Thomas Henry Withers, 'A Liassic Crab, and the Origin of the Brachyura', *Annals and Magazine of Natural History*, X/9 (1932), pp. 313–23; Reinhard Förster, '*Eocarcinus praecursor* Withers (Decapoda, Brachyura) from the Lower Pliensbachian of Yorkshire and the Early Crabs', *Neues Jahrbuch für Geologie und Paläontologie, Monatshefte*, I (1979), pp. 15–27; Joachim T. Haug and Carolin Haug, 'Eoprosopon kluge (Brachyura) – The Oldest Unequivocal and Most "Primitive" Crab Reconsidered', *Palaeodiversity*, VII (2014), pp. 149–58.

15 Adiël A. Klompmaker, 'Extreme Diversity of Decapod Crustaceans from the mid-Cretaceous (late Albian) of Spain: Implications for Cretaceous Decapod Paleoecology', *Cretaceous Research*, XLI (April 2013), pp. 150–85.

16 Adiël A. Klompmaker, Roger W. Portell and Sancia E. T. van der Meij, 'Trace Fossil Evidence of Coral-inhabiting Crabs (Cryptochiridae) and its Implications for Growth and Paleobiogeography', www.nature.com, 24 March 2016.

17 Jeff Hecht, 'Zoologger: The Tasty Crab That Looks Like an Ugly Frog', www.newscientist.com, 7 January 2015.

18 'Shell-breaking Crabs Lived 20 Million Years Earlier Than Thought', www.sciencedaily.com, 23 April 2008.

19 Aristos Georgiou, 'Callichimaera Perplexa: Bizarre "Platypus of the Crab World" Discovered from 95 Million Years Ago', www.newsweek.com, 24 April 2019.

2 CLASSIFYING CRABS

1 Peter Castro, 'Professor Danièle Guinot', in *Crustaceana Monographs XI: Studies on Brachyura: A Homage to Danièle Guinot*, ed. Peter Castro et al. (Leiden, 2010), pp. 7–13.

2 Rafael Lemaitre, 'Patsy Ann McLaughlin, May 27, 1932–April 4, 2011', *Journal of Crustacean Biology*, XXXII/6 (2012), pp. 991–1,002.

3 Aristotle, *The History of Animals: Book IV, Part 1* [*c.* 350 BCE], available at http://classics.mit.edu, accessed 3 July 2019.

4 G. F. Warner, *The Biology of Crabs* (London, 1977), p. xiii; Peter K. L. Ng, Danièle Guinot and Peter J. F. Davie, 'Systema Brachyurorum: Part I. An Annotated Checklist of Extant Brachyuran Crabs of the World', *Raffles Bulletin of Zoology*, XVIII (2008), pp. 1–286.

5 Dorothy E. Bliss, 'General Preface', in Bliss, ed.-in-chief, *The Biology of Crustacea*, vol. I: *Systematics, the Fossil Record, and Biogeography*, ed. Lawrence G. Abele (New York, 1982), p. xiii; see also Abele, 'Preface to Volume I', p. xvii.

6 Quoted in Frederick R. Schram, 'The Fossil Record and Evolution of Crustacea', in *Systematics, the Fossil Record, and Biogeography*, ed. Abele, p. 94.

7 Benedict did little work on Brachyura; most of his research involved annelid worms and Anomura. See correspondence from Waldo L. Schmitt to Dr Edward T. James, editor of *Notable American*

148

Women, 1607–1950, 30 April 1965, in Smithsonian Institution
Archives, Record Unit 7231, Waldo L. Schmitt Papers (hereafter
Schmitt Papers), Box 73, Folder 16; see also Waldo L. Schmitt, 'Mary
J. Rathbun, 1860–1943', *Crustaceana*, XXIV/3 (1973), pp. 283–97,
cited from page proofs in Schmitt Papers, Box 73, Folder 17.

8　See Patsy A. McLaughlin and Sandra Gilchrist, 'Women's
Contributions to Carcinology', in *History of Carcinology*, ed. Frank
Truesdale (Rotterdam, 1993), pp. 165–206; Richard Conniff, *House
of Lost Worlds: Dinosaurs, Dynasties, and the Story of Life on Earth*
(New Haven, CT, 2016), pp. 120–22; L. B. Holthius and R. W. Ingle,
'Isabella Gordon, DSC, OBE – 1901–1988', *Crustaceana*, LVI/1 (1989),
pp. 93–105.

9　The work was published in three parts: Mary J. Rathbun, 'Les
crabs d'eau douce (Potamonidae)', in *Nouvelles archives du Muséum
d'histoire naturelle*, Series 4, VI/1 (Paris, 1904), pp. 225–312; VII/2
(1905), pp. 159–323; VIII/3 (1906), pp. 33–122.

10　Mary J. Rathbun, 'The Grapsoid Crabs of America', *Smithsonian
Institution/United States National Museum Bulletin*, XCVII
(Washington, DC, 1918); Rathbun, 'The Spider Crabs of America',
Smithsonian Institution/United States National Museum Bulletin,
CXXIX (Washington, DC, 1925); Rathbun, 'The Cancroid Crabs of
America of the Families Euryalidae, Portunidae, Atelecyclidae,
Cancridae, and Xanthidae', *Smithsonian Institution/United States
National Museum Bulletin*, CLII (Washington, DC, 1918); Rathbun,
'The Oxystomatous and Allied Crabs of America', *Smithsonian
Institution/United States National Museum Bulletin*, CLXVI
(Washington, DC, 1937).

11　Mary J. Rathbun, 'A New Species of Pinnotherid Crab from
Costa Rica', *Journal of the Washington Academy of Sciences*, XXI
(1931), p. 262 (typed manuscript), in Smithsonian Institution
Archives, Record Unit 7256, Mary Jane Rathbun Papers, 1860–1943
(hereafter Rathbun Papers), Box 3, Folder 16.

12　Mary J. Rathbun, 'New Species of Fossil Raninidae from Oregon',
Journal of the Washington Academy of Sciences, XXII (1932), pp.
239–42 (typed manuscript), in Rathbun Papers, Box 3, Folder 18.

13 Mary J. Rathbun, 'Reports on the Scientific Results of an Expedition to Rain Forest Remnants in Uganda and Kenya', *Bulletin of the Museum of Comparative Zoology at Harvard College*, LXXIX (1935), pp. 23–8 (handwritten and typed manuscripts), in Rathbun papers, Box 3, Folder 30.

14 Correspondence from Maury to Rathbun, 13 October 1926, in Rathbun Papers, Box 2, Folder 8: Maury, Carlotta J., 1923, 1926–31, 1936.

15 Correspondence from Rathbun to Maury, 26 October 1926, ibid.

16 Correspondence from Rathbun to Maury, 9 December 1926 (handwritten note), ibid.

17 Correspondence from Maury to Rathbun, 13 August 1927, ibid.

18 Correspondence from Rathbun to Maury, 27 January 1931 (carbon copy), ibid.

19 Correspondence from Maury to Rathbun, 1 February 1931 (handwritten note); also, from Maury to Rathbun, 13 February 1931 (typed), ibid.

20 Correspondence from Rathbun to Maury, 25 May 1936 (carbon copy), ibid.

21 Correspondence from Maury to Rathbun, 26 May 1936, ibid.

22 Correspondence from Rathbun to Prof. Hubert Lyman Clark, 8 February 1928 (carbon copy), in Rathbun Papers, Box 8, Folder 12.

23 See correspondence from Schmitt to James, 30 April 1965, in Schmitt Papers, Box 73, Folder 16; see also Schmitt, 'The [illegible] exhibit' (handwritten note), in Schmitt Papers, Box 74, Folder 3: Mary Jane Rathbun – Miscellaneous Notes.

24 Mary J. Rathbun, 'The Genus Callinectes', *Proceedings of the United States National Museum*, XVIII (1896), pp. 349–75 plus plates. Later authors determined that blue crabs found along North and South American coasts belong to different species.

25 'Koch Industries: Secretly Funding the Climate Denial Machine', www.greenpeace.org, accessed 25 July 2019.

26 Enrique Macpherson, William Jones and Michel Segonac, 'A New Squat Lobster Family of Galatheoida (Crustacea,

Decapoda, Anomura) from the Hydrothermal Vents of the
Pacific-Antarctic Ridge', *Zoosystema*, XXVII/4 (2005), pp. 709–23.

27 Andrew R. Thurber, William J. Jones and Kareen Schnabel,
'Dancing for Food in the Deep Sea: Bacterial Farming by a New
Species of Yeti Crab', *PLOS ONE*, VI/11 (2011).

28 Sven Thatje et al., 'Adaptations to Hydrothermal Vent Life in Kiwa
tyleri, a New Species of Yeti Crab from the East Scotia Ridge,
Antarctica', *PLOS ONE*, X/6 (2015).

29 Appukuttannair Biju Kumar, Smrithy Raj and Peter K. L. Ng,
'Description of a New Genus and New Species of a Fully Arboreal
Crab (Decapoda: Brachyura: Gecarcinucidae) from the Western
Ghats, India, with Notes on the Ecology of Arboreal Crabs', *Journal
of Crustacean Biology*, XXXVII/2 (2017), pp. 157–67.

30 'Exposed: Live Hermit Crabs' Shells Crushed, Hundreds Dead at
Pet Trade Supplier', http://peta.org, accessed 17 July 2019.

31 J. R. Henderson, 'Report on the Anomura collected by HMS
Challenger During the Years 1873–1876', in *Report on the Scientific
Results of the Voyage of the HMS Challenger During the Years 1873–76:
Zoology*, vol. XXVII, ed. Sir C. Wyville Thomson and John Murray
(London, 1888), pp. i–221.

32 Rafael Lemaitre, Dwi Listyo Rahayu and Tomoyuki Komai,
'A Revision of "Blanket-hermit Crabs" of the Genus *Paguropsis*
Henderson 1888, with the Description of a New Genus and Five
New Species (Crustacea, Anomura, Diogenidae)', *ZooKeys*, DCCLII
(2018), pp. 17–97.

33 Phone interview with the author, 17 July 2019.

34 Javier Luque et al., 'Exceptional Preservation of Mid-Cretaceous
Marine Arthropods and the Evolution of Novel Forms via
Heterochrony', *Science Advances*, V/4 (2019).

35 Lindsey Bever, 'Newly Discovered "Beautiful Nightmare" Crab Had
Wrench-like Claws and Enormous, Cartoonish Eyes', *Washington
Post*, 26 April 2019.

36 Email correspondence from Javier Luque to the author, 8 June 2019.

37 See Amanda Jackson, 'It's the Size of a Quarter, with Big, Bug Eyes:
And It's the Strangest Crab That Ever Lived', www.cnn.com,

25 April 2019; 'Canadian Scientists Help Unearth "Utterly Bizarre" Chimera Crab Fossil', *The Telegram* [St John's, Newfoundland], 24 April 2018; '"Rule-breaking" Crab Fossils Have Weird Shrimp and Lobster Features', www.newscientist.com, 24 April 2019; Lindsey Bever, 'This 90-million-year-old Crab Chimera Is a Beautiful Mess of an Animal', www.sciencealert.com, 25 April 2019.

3 ARE CRABS CRABBY?

1 William W. Warner, *Beautiful Swimmers: Watermen, Crabs and the Chesapeake Bay* [1976] (New York, 1994), p. 270.
2 Sam Langford, 'The Hill I Will Die On: Cancer Is the Worst Zodiac Sign', www.junkee.com, 27 September 2018.
3 John Barth, 'Historical Fiction, Fictitious History, and Chesapeake Bay Blue Crabs, or, About Aboutness', *Washington Post*, 15 July 1979.
4 Joel W. Martin, 'The Samurai Crab', *Terra*, XXXI/4 (1991).
5 Peter A. Biro and Judy A. Stamps, 'Are Animal Personality Traits Linked to Life-history Productivity?', *Trends in Ecology and Evolution*, XXIII/7 (2008), pp. 361–8.
6 Jeremy Bentham, *An Introduction to the Principles of Morals and Legislation* (London, 1789).
7 Barry Magee and Robert W. Elwood, 'Shock Avoidance by Discrimination Learning in the Shore Crab (*Carcinus maenas*) Is Consistent with a Key Criterion for Pain', *Journal of Experimental Biology*, CCXVI (2013), pp. 353–8. Magee and Elwood cite definitions of pain in animals in M. Zimmerman, 'Physiological Mechanisms of Pain and Its Treatment,' *Klin. Anasthesiol. Intensivther* (1986), and L. U. Sneddon, 'Pain Perception in Fish: Indicators and Endpoints', *Institute for Laboratory Animal Research Journal*, L (2009), pp. 338–42.
8 Katsushi Sakai, Michael Türkay and Si-Liang Yang, 'Revision of the *Helice/Chasmagnathus* Complex (Crustacea: Decapoda: Brachyura)', *Abhandlungen der senckenbergischen naturforschenden Gesellschaft*, DCXV (2006), pp. 1–76.

9   See María del Valle Fathala et al., 'A Field Model of Learning: 1.
    Short-term memory in the Crab *Chasmagathus granulatus*', *Journal
    of Comparative Physiology A*, CXCVI (2010), pp. 61–75; also, María
    del Valle Fathala, M. C. Kunert and H. Maldonado, 'A Field Model
    of Learning: 2. Long-term Memory in the Crab *Chasmagathus
    granulatus*', ibid., pp. 77–84.

10 Chloe A. Raderschall, Robert D. Magrath and Jan M. Hemmi,
    'Habituation under Natural Conditions: Model Predators Are
    Distinguished by Approach Direction', *Journal of Experimental
    Biology*, CCXIV (2011), pp. 4,209–18.

11 Ross J. Roudez, Terry Glover and Judith S. Weis, 'Learning in
    an Invasive and a Native Predatory Crab', *Biological Invasions*, X
    (2008), pp. 1,191–6.

4   IF IT WALKS LIKE A CRAB . . .

1   Jack Kroll, 'DeNiro: A Star for the '70s', *Newsweek*, 16 May 1977,
    p. 83; Gilles Deleuze and Felix Guattari made much of the
    statement within the 'Becoming-Intense, Becoming-Animal,
    Becoming-Imperceptible . . .' section of *A Thousand Plateaus:
    Capitalism and Schizophrenia* (Minneapolis, MN, 1987), pp. 274–5.

2   René Descartes, *The Philosophical Writings of Descartes, Vol. III:
    The Correspondence*, trans. John Cottingham, Robert Stoothoff,
    Dugald Murdoch and Anthony Kenny (Cambridge, 1991), pp. 181
    and 234.

3   Jennifer R. A. Taylor, Jack Hebrank and William M. Kier,
    'Mechanical Properties of the Rigid and Hydrostatic Skeletons
    of Molting Blue Crabs, *Callinectes sapidus* Rathbun', *Journal of
    Experimental Biology*, CCX (2007), pp. 4,272–8.

4   Patricia Ruth Yvonne Backwell, 'Synchronous Waving in Fiddler
    Crabs: A Review', *Current Zoology*, LXV/1 (2019), pp. 83–8.

5   Richard N. C. Milner, Michael D. Jennions and Patricia R. Y.
    Backwell, 'Eavesdropping in Crabs: An Agency for Lady Detection',
    Biology Letters, VI (2010), pp. 755–7.

6   Kenneth P. Oakley, *Man the Tool-maker*, 5th edn (London, 1961).

7 On the singularity of boxer crab tool use, see Martin Haywood and
   Sue Wells, *The Manual of Marine Invertebrates* (Morris Plains, NJ,
   1989); see also Julian K. Finn, Tom Tregenza and Mark D. Norman,
   'Defensive Tool Use in a Coconut-carrying Octopus', *Current
   Biology*, XIX/23 (2009).

8 Ming-Shiou Jeng, 'Newly Recorded Symbiotic Crabs (Crustacea:
   Decapoda: Brachyura) from Southern Taiwan Coral Reefs',
   Zoological Studies, XXXIII/4 (1994), pp. 314–18.

9 Karl August Möbius, Ferdinand Richters and Eduard von Martens,
   Beiträge zur Meeresfauna der Insel Mauritius und der Seychelles
   (Berlin, 1880), cited in J. E. Duerden, 'On the Habits and Reactions
   of Crabs Bearing Actinians in Their Claws,' in *Proceedings of the
   General Meetings for Scientific Business of the Zoological Society of
   London I* (London, 1905), pp. 494–511.

10 Ibid., p. 500.

11 Robert Lamb, 'Boxer Crabs Clone Their Anemone Bioweapons',
   https://animals.howstuffworks.com, 31 January 2017.

12 Schnytzer collected limited numbers of *L. leptochelis* with
   permits from the Israeli National Parks Authority, and returned
   these subjects to the same shores where they were found. Other
   boxer species – rarer, living at greater depths – he says, are
   even more difficult to study. Personal email correspondence,
   20 May 2019.

13 Yisrael Schnytzer et al., 'Boxer Crabs Induce Asexual Reproduction
   of their Associate Sea Anemones by Splitting and Intraspecific
   Theft', *PeerJ*, 5:e2954 (31 January 2017).

14 Yisrael Schnytzer et al., 'Bonsai Anemones: Growth Suppression
   of Sea Anemones by Their Associated Kleptoparasitic Boxer Crab',
   Journal of Experimental Marine Biology and Ecology, 448 (2013), pp.
   265–70.

15 Simona Weinglass, 'Meet the Israeli Crab That Crawled Out
   from Under a Rock to Global Stardom', *The Times of Israel*,
   21 March 2017.

16 Graeme D. Ruxton and Martin Stevens, 'The Evolutionary
   Ecology of Decorating Behaviour', *Biology Letters*, XI (2015).

17 H. C. Stevens, 'Acquired Specific Reactions to Color
(Chromotropism) in *Oregonia gracilis*', *Journal of Animal Behavior*,
III/4 (1913), p. 153.

18 On 'planting out', see Geoffrey Smith, 'Crustacea and Arachnids,'
in *The Cambridge Natural History*, IV (London, 1909), p. 192;
also J. S. Kingsley, 'Crustacea and Insects', *Riverside Natural
History*, II (Boston, MA, and New York, 1888), p. 61, both cited
in Stevens, 'Acquired Specific Reactions to Color', pp. 150–51.

19 Kingsley, 'Crustacea and Insects', p. 61.

20 Stevens, 'Acquired Specific Reactions to Color', p. 174.

21 John J. Stachowicz and Mark E. Hay, 'Reducing Predation
Through Chemically Mediated Camouflage: Indirect Effects of
Plant Defenses on Herbivores', *Ecology*, LXXX/2 (1999),
pp. 495–509.

5 A DEADLY CATCH?

1 Brett Hambright, 'Man's Appetite for Crab Legs Sparks Alleged
Assault at All-you-can-eat Buffet', www.lancasteronline.com,
16 May 2012.

2 Ruth Brown, '2 Arrested for Brawl at Buffet over Crab Legs',
New York Post, 27 February 2019.

3 Food and Agriculture Organization of the United Nations,
Globefish Highlights: A Quarterly Update on World Seafood Markets
(Rome, 2019), pp. 63–4.

4 'Noma: A Review of the Seafood Season Menu', https://
scallionpancake.com, 30 April 2019; see also https://noma.dk.

5 J. R. Minkel, 'Earliest Known Seafood Dinner Discovered',
Scientific American, 17 October 2007.

6 Robert C. Walter et al., 'Early Human Occupation of the Red
Sea Coast off Eritrea During the Last Interglacial', *Nature*, CDV
(4 May 2000), pp. 65–9.

7 Torben C. Rick et al., 'Archaeology, Taphonomy, and Historical
Ecology of Chesapeake Bay Blue Crabs (*Callinectes sapidus*)',
Journal of Archaeological Science, LV (2015), pp. 42–54.

8 Lynne Olver's *Food Timeline: FAQs: Fish and Shellfish* contains links to many digitized cookbooks and other sources: www. foodtimeline.org/foodlobster.html#crab, accessed 17 June 2019.

9 Victor Reklaitis, 'James McMenamin: In Crabtown, He Was King', www.dailypress.com, 28 August 2006.

10 Jolene Thym, 'Taste-off: The Best Canned Crab – and Nastiest', www.mercurynews.com, 11 November 2015; see also Lauren Sommer, 'Why a Neurotoxin Is Closing Crab Season in California', www.npr.org, 7 November 2015.

11 Leviticus 11:9–11, *The Holy Bible: Old and New Testaments*, Revised Standard Version (possibly 1901), cited in Mary Douglas, *Purity and Danger* [1966] (Oxon, UK, and New York, 2002), p. 53.

12 See Douglas, *Purity and Danger*, pp. 55–6.

13 Ibid., pp. 54–6.

14 María Pedrosa et al., 'Shellfish Allergy: A Comprehensive Review', *Clinical Reviews in Allergy and Immunology*, XLIX (2015), pp. 203–16.

15 Chee K. Woo and Ami L. Bahna, 'Not All Shellfish "Allergy" Is Allergy!', *Clinical and Translational Allergy*, 1/3 (2011).

16 Benoit Vidal-Firaud and Denis Chateau/Food and Agriculture Organization of the United Nations, *World Surimi Market – Globefish Research Programme*, LXXXIX (Rome, 2007), p. 1.

17 Becky Manfield, '"Imitation Crab" and the Material Culture of Commodity Production', *Cultural Geographies*, X (2003), pp. 176–95. The U.S.- and Japan-based seafood companies Berelson and Sugiyo brought surimi to American markets in a joint venture.

18 Tom Seaman, 'Pollock Surimi "Can't Meet Global Demand" as Tropical Supply Continues to Drop', www.undercurrentnews.com, 10 December 2018.

19 John M. Kelso, 'Potential Food Allergens in Medications', *Clinical Reviews in Allergy and Immunology*, CXXXIII (2014), p. 1,513.

20 Sarah Zhang, 'The Last Days of the Blue-blood Harvest', www.theatlantic.com, 9 May 2018.

21 William W. Warner, *Beautiful Swimmers: Watermen, Crabs and the Chesapeake Bay* [1976] (New York, 1994).

22 David Griffith, 'New Immigrants in an Old Industry: Mexican
    H-2B Workers in the mid-Atlantic Blue Crab Processing Industry',
    Changing Face, III (1997), available at http://migration.ucdavis.
    edu/cf.

23 Ian Burke, 'Why This Maryland Island Town Is Called "Isla de las
    Mexicanas"', www.saveur.com, 24 May 2017.

24 Amy Lu, 'No Visas, No Workers, No Business for Maryland's Crab
    Industry', www.wboc.com, 3 April 2018.

25 Ryan Marshall, 'Crabmeat Industry Hit Hard by Lack of Workers',
    Daily Times (Salisbury, MD), 4 May 2018; Brooke Butler, 'Crab
    Company Reacts to Dept. of Homeland Security's Finalization of
    H-2B Visa Increase', www.wmdt.com, 6 May 2019.

26 Daniel Costa, 'The H-2B Temporary Foreign Worker Program'
    (testimony before the U.S. Senate Subcommittee on Immigration
    and the National Interest, 6 June 2016), available at www.epi.org.

27 International Human Rights Law Clinic at American University
    Washington College of Law and Centro de los Derechos del
    Migrante, Inc., *Picked Apart: The Hidden Struggles of Migrant Worker
    Women in the Maryland Crab Industry* (Washington, DC, 2010);
    Thurka Sangaramoorthy, 'Hooper's Island: The Place That Time
    Forgot', www.thurkasangaramoorthy.com, 6 September 2015.

28 André Cartier et al., 'Prevalence of Crab Asthma in Crab Plant
    Workers in Newfoundland and Labrador', *International Journal
    of Circumpolar Health*, LXIII/2 (2004), pp. 333–6. This figure is
    consistent with the findings of a study showing 15.6 per cent of
    workers with symptoms of snow crab asthma in processing plants
    in Quebec; see André Cartier et al., 'Occupational Asthmas in
    Snow Crab-processing Workers', *Journal of Allergy and Clinical
    Immunology*, LXXIV/3 (1984), pp. 261–9.

29 Jakob Hjort Bønløkke et al., 'Snow Crab Allergy and Asthma
    Among Greenlandic Workers – A Pilot Study', *International Journal
    of Circumpolar Health*, LXXI (2012).

30 See Jill Jarocha, 'Facts of the Catch: Occupational Injuries, Illnesses,
    and Fatalities to Fishing Workers, 2003–2009', *Beyond the Numbers*,
    I/9 (2012), available at http://bls.gov.

31 Alaska Department of Fish and Game, '2017–2019 King and
Tanner Crab Commercial Fishing Regulations', pp. 9 and 50, rules
5 AAC 34.060, 5 AAC 34.065, 5 AAC 35.060, 5 AAC 34.065,
www.adfg.alaska.gov, accessed 19 June 2019.

32 See Bloveslife and BlovesASMR Eating Her Way, www.youtube.com,
accessed 20 June 2019.

33 See '[ENG SUB] King Crab (Excited) *Dorothy Mukbang*',
www.youtube.com, accessed 20 June 2019.

34 See Kaneko, '1,700,000 yen ($1,500 U.S.) for One! I Tried the
World's Largest Crab "Tasmanian King Crab"!', www.youtube.com,
accessed 20 June 2019.

35 Nick Rahaim, '"Deadliest Catch"? Not Even in the Top Three',
www.salon.com, 16 May 2015; 'Despite Deadly Rep, Alaska Fishing
Safer', www.cbsnews.com, 28 March 2008.

6 A WORLD WITHOUT CRABS

1 This text overlays a photograph by the artist David Wojnarowicz
titled *What Is This Little Guy's Job in the World?* (1990), depicting
a larger-than-life-sized human hand, with a tiny animal perched
between palm and thumb. It is a frog. It might just as easily have
been a crab.

2 Yereth Rosen, 'New Maps Show Bering Sea Holds World's Most
Acidic Ocean Waters', *Anchorage Daily News*, 21 November 2014.

3 William Christopher Long et al., 'Effects of Ocean Acidification
on Juvenile Red King Crab (*Paralithodes camtschaticus*) and
Tanner Crab (*Chionoecetes bairdi*) Growth, Condition, Calcification,
and Survival', *PLOS ONE*, 4 April 2013, available at
https://journals.plos.org.

4 Chesapeake Bay Foundation Reports, *Bad Water and the Decline
of Blue Crabs in the Chesapeake Buy* (Annapolis, MD, 2008).

5 This is not to say that the area is entirely healthy. The Chesapeake
Bay Foundation (www.cbf.org) continues to fight to protect the
watershed from pollution, sewage, dangerous resource extraction,
overuse and other threats.

6 In 2011, oxygen in parts of Mobile Bay dropped for days to unheard of low levels of oxygen, less than 0.5 parts per million (ppm); it only takes a drop below 2 ppm to endanger marine animal life. See Ben Raines, 'Scientists Report Unusually Low Levels of Oxygen in Mobile Bay Waters', www.al.com, 6 September 2014.

7 United Nations, 'Global Issues: Climate Change', www.un.org, accessed 31 August 2019.

8 Between 1901 and 2010 the seas rose some 19 cm (7.5 in.) and they continue to rise at an alarming rate: www.un.org, accessed 28 August 2019.

9 H. L. Clark and P.R.Y. Backwell, 'Micro-climate and Incubation in a Fiddler Crab Species', *Journal of Experimental Marine Biology and Ecology*, CDLXXXV (2016), pp. 18–23.

10 Erik Kristensen, 'Mangrove Crabs as Ecosystem Engineers; With Emphasis on Sediment Processes', *Journal of Sea Research*, LIX (2008), pp. 30–43.

11 Stephen M. Smith, 'Vegetation Change in the Salt Marshes of Cape Cod National Seashore (Massachusetts, USA) Between 1984 and 2013', *Wetlands*, XXXV/1 (2014).

12 Stephen M. Smith, Megan C. Tyrrell and Melanie Congretel, 'Palatability of Salt Marsh Forbs and Grasses to the Purple Marsh Crab (*Sesarma reticulatum*) and the Potential for Re-vegetation of Herbivory-induced Salt Marsh Dieback Areas in Cape Cod (Massachusetts, USA)', *Wetlands Ecology and Management*, XXI (2013), pp. 263–75.

13 Stephen M. Smith and Megan C. Tyrrell, 'Effects of Mud Fiddler Crabs (*Uca pugnax*) on the Recruitment of Halophyte Seedlings in Salt Marsh Dieback Areas of Cape Cod (Massachusetts, USA)', *Ecological Research*, XXVII (2012), p. 235.

14 Ibid., pp. 233–7.

15 Tyler C. Coverdale et al., 'New England Salt Marsh Recovery: Opportunistic Colonization of an Invasive Species and Its Non-consumptive Effects', *PLOS ONE*, VIII/8 (2013), available at www.plosone.org.

16 Jesús A. Ballesteros and Prashant P. Sharma, 'A Critical Appraisal of the Placement of Xiphosura (Chelicerata) with Account of Known Sources of Phylogenetic Error', *Systematic Biology* (27 March 2019), available at www.academic.oup.edu.

17 Atlantic State Marine Fisheries Commission, *2019 Horseshoe Crab Benchmark Stock Assessment and Peer Review Report* (Arlington, VA, 2019), available at www.asmfc.org.

18 There is reason to be optimistic that fewer horseshoe crabs may be harvested in coming years: in 2018, the U.S. Food and Drug Administration allowed the pharmaceutical manufacturer Lonza to use a synthetic product known as the recombinant Factor C Assay, to test for endotoxins in a new migraine drug. Expanded use of a test produced without animal products will help protect the American horseshoe crab, as well as related Asian species that are in even more serious decline. See 'FDA Approves First Drug Using the Recombinant Factor C Assay for Endotoxin Testing', www.biopharmadive.com, 8 November 2018.

Select Bibliography

Bliss, Dorothy E., *Shrimps, Lobsters and Crabs: Their Fascinating Life Story* (New York, 1990)

Cramer, Deborah, *The Narrow Edge: A Tiny Bird, An Ancient Crab and an Epic Journey* (New Haven, CT, 2015)

Crane, Jocelyn, *Fiddler Crabs of the World: Ocypodidae: Genus Uca* (Princeton, NJ, 1975)

Fortey, Richard, *Horseshoe Crabs and Velvet Worms: The Story of the Animals and Plants That Time Has Left Behind* (New York, 2012)

Fredericks, Anthony D., *Horseshoe Crab: Biography of a Survivor* (Washington, DC, 2012)

Hughes, Ted, 'Ghost Crabs', in *Wodwo* (London, 1967), pp. 21–2

Kirby, Lisa A., 'Cowboys of the High Seas: Representations of Working-class Masculinity on *Deadliest Catch*', *Journal of Popular Culture*, XLVI/1 (2013), pp. 109–18

Michener, James A., *Chesapeake* (New York, 1978)

Moore, Lisa Jean, *Catch and Release: The Enduring Yet Vulnerable Horseshoe Crab* (New York, 2017)

Ng, Peter et al., *Studies on Brachyura: A Homage to Danièle Guinot* (Leiden, 2010)

Sargent, William, *Crab Wars: A Tale of Crabs, Bioterrorism, and Human Health* (Hanover, NH, 2006)

Truesdale, Frank, ed., *Crustacean Issues 8: History of Carcinology* (Rotterdam and Brookfield, VT, 1993)

Warner, William W., *Beautiful Swimmers: Watermen, Crabs and the Chesapeake Bay* (New York, 1976)

Weis, Judith S., *Walking Sideways: The Remarkable World of Crabs* (Ithaca, NY, 2012)

—, and Carol A. Butler, *Salt Marshes: A Natural and Unnatural History* (New Brunswick, NJ, 2009)

Wilkins, Kelli A., *Hermit Crabs for Dummies* (Hoboken, NJ, 2007)

Associations and Websites

ALASKA BERING SEA CRABBERS
4005 20th Avenue West, Suite 102
Seattle, WA 98199, USA
www.alaskaberingseacrabbers.org

CARCINOLOGICAL SOCIETY OF JAPAN
Department of Environmental Management Engineering
Okayama University
3-1-1 Tsushima-naka
Okayama 700-8530, Japan
http://csjenglish.webnode.jp

CENSUS OF MARINE LIFE
Consortium for Ocean Leadership
1201 New York Avenue NW, Suite 420
Washington, DC 20005, USA
www.coml.org

CHESAPEAKE BAY FOUNDATION
Philip Merrill Environmental Center
6 Herndon Avenue
Annapolis, MD 21403, USA
www.cbf.org

THE CRUSTACEAN SOCIETY
950 Herndon Parkway, Suite 450
Herndon, VA 20170, USA
www.thecrustaceansociety.org

CRUSTACEANA: INTERNATIONAL JOURNAL OF CRUSTACEAN RESEARCH
https://brill.com/cr

FIDDLER CRABS
Blog by Michael S. Rosenberg, Center for the Study of Biological
Complexity, Virginia Commonwealth University
www.fiddlercrab.info

INVASIVE SPECIES COMPENDIUM
CAB International
Wallingford
Oxon OX10 8DE, UK
www.cabi.org/isc

MARINE BIOLOGICAL LABORATORY
7 MBL Street
Woods Hole, MA 02543, USA
www.mbl.edu

NOAA fisheries/National Marine Fisheries Service
National Oceanic and Atmospheric Administration
1315 East-West Highway
Silver Spring, MD 20910, USA
www.fisheries.noaa.gov

NORTH CAROLINA FISHERIES ASSOCIATION
101 N. 5th Street
Morehead City, NC 28557, USA
https://ncfish.org

OKINAWA NATURE PHOTOGRAPHY BY SHAWN MILLER
https://okinawanaturephotography.com

ORIANA POINDEXTER (artist, scientist, free diver and surfer)
www.orianapoindexter.com

POLAR RESEARCH INSTITUTE OF MARINE FISHERIES AND
OCEANOGRAPHY
6 Akademika Knipovicha St.
Murmansk 183038, Russia
www.pinro.ru

SCRIPPS INSTITUTE OF OCEANOGRAPHY
9500 Gilman Drive
La Jolla, CA 92093, USA
https://scripps.ucsd.edu

SEA CHANGE TRUST
Cape Town, South Africa
https://seachangeproject.com

SEAFOOD WATCH
Monterey Bay Aquarium Foundation
886 Cannery Row
Monterey, CA 93940, USA
www.seafoodwatch.org

SMITHSONIAN INSTITUTION
Department of Invertebrate Zoology
National Museum of Natural History
10th Street and Constitution Avenue Northwest
Washington, DC 20560
https://naturalhistory.si.edu/research/invertebrate-zoology

SOCIEDADE BRASILEIRA DE CARCINOLOGIA
Universidade Sagrado Coração
USC Laboratório de Sistemática Zoológica
Rua Irmã Arminda, 10–50
Brasil 17011-160 Bauru, São Paulo, Brazil
https://crustacea.org.br/en

WOODS HOLE OCEANOGRAPHIC INSTITUTION
266 Woods Hole Road
Woods Hole, MA 02543, USA
www.whoi.edu

Acknowledgements

This project has been a labour of love, one that I stumbled into just as surely I stumbled into a colony of hermit crabs crossing a beach in Costa Rica. It was a pleasure to approach the crab's corner of the animal world from the perspective of a curious outsider, and to have found so many people who work with crabs such generous conversationalists and correspondents. My thanks go to those that I called upon while I worked on *Crab*, including Heather Bracken-Grissom, Rafael Lemaitre, Javier Luque, Curtis Marean, Yisrael Schnytzer and Jennifer Taylor; Karen Reed for giving me a behind-the-scenes tour of the Smithsonian Institution's Museum Support Center; Teddy Kavros of the Hampton History Museum, Virginia; and the staff of the Smithsonian Institution Archives, especially Tad Bennicoff and Heidi Stover.

I consider myself lucky to have had opportunities to get out into the field with Stephen Smith, Plant Ecologist for the National Park Service Cape Cod National Seashore; a team led by Janet Drohan and organized by Christopher Green, Volunteer Coordinator for Wellfleet Bay Wildlife Sanctuary, Mass Audubon; and Kathy Garofalo and José Ramírez-Garofalo, conducting horseshoe crab surveys at Gateway National Recreation Area, Staten Island, New York. Charlotte Seid, Museum Scientist and Collection Manager at Scripps Institute of Oceanography, went the extra mile in hosting my tour of the Oceanographic Collections at Scripps, as well as connecting me with artists whose work appears in this volume, to whom I am also very grateful. Friends and colleagues including David Gerstner, Kate Horsfield, Eliza Kentridge, Edward Miller, Debbie Nadolney, Jason Simon and Jay Winter shared literary crabs, crab artefacts and crab anecdotes.

Warm thanks to the people at Reaktion who made this book possible: Jonathan Burt, series editor, for his faith in my work and his role in creating the marvellous Animal series, as well as publisher Michael Leaman, Alexandru Ciobanu, Phoebe Colley, Susannah Jayes, Rebecca Ratnayake and Amy Salter.

And I owe special debts of gratitude to a few humans whose help was vital. Mitchell Lovell and Steve Hager provided technical support. Limnologist Jeff Mantus, Lisa Sette of the Center for Coastal Studies in Provincetown, Massachusetts, and Pat Backwell of the Research School of Biology at Australian National University (ANU), were generous enough to read chapters in draft form. My conversations with Pat were richly inspiring; I was fortunate to be able to meet with her in person while a Visiting Fellow at the Humanities Research Centre (HRC) at ANU. Thanks to both the HRC for its support of my work on representations of animals in times of crisis, and the College of Staten Island, which provided me with a sabbatical that allowed me to focus on these projects. Lisa Sette, Elizabeth Bradfield and Tony Freitas encouraged me to take up this project, and I'm glad they did. Finally, Arlene Stein never seemed to tire of my endless stories of these crabs: you are my best reader.

Photo Acknowledgements

The author and the publishers wish to express their thanks to the below sources of illustrative material and/or permission to reproduce it.

123rf.com: pp. 8 (Charles Wollertz), 115 (Kesinee Srisura), 143 (Brian Lasenby); Cynthia Chris: pp. 12, 16, 19, 39 left and right, 49, 100, 103, 110, 134, 138, 139, 140, 141, 145 centre; Tanya Detto: pp. 84, 85, 87, 130; Estonian Museum of Natural History: p. 18; Freshwater and Marine Image Bank, University of Washington Libraries: pp. 24, 47, 73, 77 top right, 82, 94, 145 top left; Amanda Gannon: p. 11 top and bottom; courtesy of the Hampton History Museum: pp. 104 (2012.45.1:43), 105 (x.1376.8), 145 top right (2012.45.6); Hermitage Museum, St Petersburg: p. 107; Kate Horsfield: pp. 60, 80, 83; Jannes Landschoff: p. 48; Library of Congress, Washington, DC: pp. 29 top right, 58; Barry Magee: p. 72; Metropolitan Museum of Art, New York: pp. 56, 59, 77 bottom left, 81, 108, 128; Shawn Miller: p. 127; Museum Boijmans Van Beuningen, Rotterdam: p. 31; Museum of Fine Arts, Houston: p. 106; Paul Ng: pp. 44, 145 bottom right; Oriana Poindexter (www.orianapoindexter.com): pp. 68, 102; Public Health Image Library, U.S. Centers for Disease Control: p. 17; Tanya L. Rogers: p. 76; Courtesy of Yisrael Schnytzer: pp. 90, 92, 93, 98; Scripps Institution of Oceanography Benthic Invertebrate Collection, San Diego: pp. 13 (Charlotte Seid (SIO)), 41(Greg Rouse (SIO)), 42 (Greg Rouse (SIO) and the Schmidt Ocean Institute), 52 (Laboratory of Greg Rouse (SIO)), 144 bottom right (Greg Rouse (SIO)); Charlotte Seid: pp. 10 left and right, 26, 124; Shutterstock: pp. 15 (Rattiya Thongdumhyu), 111 (Muk Photo), 114 (Brent Hofacker); Lily Simonson: p. 43; Smithsonian Institution Archives, Washington, DC: pp. 29 bottom, 33, 36, 37, 144 centre left; image by Oksana Vernygora, Courtesy of Javier Luque: p. 51; Wikipedia: pp. 6 (Hans Hillewaert cc 4.0), 95 (Dan Hershman cc 2.0), 97 (Ed Bierman cc 2.0), 144 top left (David Goehring cc 2.0).

Index

Page numbers in *italics* refer to illustrations

Alcock, Alfred William 46–7
Alfred P. Sloan Foundation 40
allergies to shellfish 112–14, 116
Andersen, Hans Christian 60
Anomura 9–10, 12–13, 20–21,
  23, 29
  see also hermit crabs
Aristophanes 79
Aristotle 29, 53
Attack of the Crab Monsters 62–3,
  63

Backwell, Patricia 69, 87–8
Bang, Fred 116
Barth, John 55, 64
Bateson, Gregory
Beers, Thom 119
Benedict, James L. 32
Bentham, Jeremy 70
Błażejowski, Błażej 20
Bliss, Dorothy E. 30
Borradaile, Lancelot Alexander 21
Bosc, Louis 86
Bouguereau, William-Adolphe,
  Le crabe 56, *57*

Brachyura ('true crabs') 9–10,
  12–14, 22–5, 29, *29*, 34–6,
  36, 50
Bush, Charlotte 33
Bush, Katherine J. 33
Bush, Lucy 33

Cancer (astrological sign) 55–6,
  56, 59
Cancer (constellation) 56–7
cancer (disease) 59–60
Carroll, Lewis 65
Census of Marine Life 40–41, 43
Churchill, E. P., Jr, *Life History of
  the Blue Crab* 82
Clark, Hubert Lyman 37
climate change 126, 130–32, 141–2
Convention on International
  Trade in Endangered Species
  of Wild Fauna and Flora
  (CITES) 101
Corbin, Grant 56, 78
Corman, Roger 62
crab, as food 101–5, *103*, *104*, *110*,
  111, *114*, *115*, 122–5

avoidance 110–12
in dietary supplements
116
see also surimi
crab, types
armed box crab (*Playmea gaudichaudii*) 124
bairdi (tanner) crab 120–21, 127
blanket crab 45–50, *47*, *48*
blue crab 15, 29, 38–9, *39*, 75–8, 81–4, 108, 117–19, 127–9, 134
blue minna (sand) crab 108
boxer crab 89–94, *90*, *93*, 98, *98*
brown crab *102*, 108
Callichimaera perplexa 25–6, 50–52, *50*
Callinectes reticulatus 35
coconut crab (*Birgus lotro*) 10, 12
decorator crab 48, 94–9, *94*, *95*, *96*
Dungeness crab 105, 108, *100*, *101*
European green crabs 75–8
fiddler crab 84–8, *84*, *85*, *87*, 130–35, *130*, 141–2
freshwater crab 12, 34
frog crab (family Raninidae) 23–4, 34, 50
gall crab 23–4, *24*
hairy stone crab 12
Kani maranjandun 43–5, *44*

king crab 12, *52*, 120–23, 127, 141
Metopaulias depressus 14
mole crab 10
mud crab 32–3
Neohelice (Chasmagnathus) granulatus 73–5
Pinnixa valerii 32
porcelain crab 10–11
porcupine crab (*Neolithodes grimaldii*) 38, *39*
Potamon amalerensis 35
Potamon (Geothatphusa) harvardi 34–5
purple marsh crab (*Sesarma reticulatum*) 133–5, *134*
rock crab 105
Sally Lightfoot crab (*Graspus graspus*) *143*
samurai crab (*Heike japonica*) 65–7
sand crab (*Emerita analoga*) 10
snow crab (also known as queen crab, opilio crab) 120, 127, *100*, *101*
spider crab 16, 23
stone crab 108, 141
swimming crab (*Carcinus maenas*) 71–2, 77
yeti crab (family Kiwadae) 40–45, *41*, *42*, *43*
Zanthopsis rathbunae 36
see also hermit crab
crab asthma 119
Crios 56, 59–60, 67

Dandridge, Violet 37–8
Darwin, Charles 20
Deadliest Catch, The 119–22, *120,
    121*
De Niro, Robert 79
Descartes, René 79–80
Dietl, Greg 24–5
Dixson, Danielle 98
Douglas, Mary 111–12
Duerden, James Edwin 91
Dürer, Albrecht, *Crab 31*
Durrell, Lawrence 101

Edwards, A. Milne 33
Elwood, Robert W. 71–2

Fathala, María del Valle 74
Finding Nemo 65
fishing for crab 104, *105,* 108–9,
    117, 119–22, *120, 121*
Förster, Reinhard 22
Freyberg, James, 'The Nightmare'
    54, 55

Gakutel, Yashima, *Crabs Near
    Water's Edge 77*
Gannon, Amanda, *Anatomy of a
    Crab 11*
Genet, Jean 18
Goodall, Jane 89
Gordon, Isabella 33
Guinot, Daniéle 22, 28–9, 53

Hall, Sidney, *Cancer 58,* 59
Harris, Captain Phil 121–2

Haug, Joachim, and Carolin 22
Hay, Mark E. 96
Heda, Willem Claesz., *Breakfast
    with a Crab 107*
Hedgpeth, Joel Walker 30, 53
Henderson, J. R. 46–7
hermit crab 14–16, 26, 28, 45
    blueberry hermit crab
    (*Coenbita purpureus*) *127*
    Clibanarius fonticola 12
    Diogenes heteropsammicola
    46
    Ecuadorian or Pacific
    hermit crab (*Coenbita
    compressus*) 7–9, *7, 8, 13*
    white-spotted hermit crab
    (*Dardanus megistos*) 26
Hippocrates 59–60
Hirohito, Emperor 33
Hokusai, Katsushika 106
    Crab and Rice Plant 108
Holder, Charles Frederick, *Along
    the Florida Reef 94*
horseshoe crabs (family
    Limulidae) 16–17, *16,*
    19–20, *19, 83,* 135–41, *138,
    139, 141*
    as source of pharmaceutical
    products 116, 136
Huxley, Julian 66–7
Huxley, Thomas 20

Jake and the Never Land Pirates
    65, *65*
jubilee 129

Karka 59
Karkinos 56, 59, 67
Kin, Adrian 20
Koch, Charles 39
Koch, David H. 38–9
Krabs, Mr (in *SpongeBob
SquarePants*) 61, 62, 67

LeMaitre, Rafael 46–50, 53
Luque, Javier 23–5, 50–53

McLaughlin, Patsy A. (Pat) 29,
46–7, 53
McMenamin, James 105
Magee, Barry 71–2
Marine Biological Laboratory
28, 116
Martin, Joel 66
mating 86–8, 130–31
Maury, Carlotta J. 35–6, 53
memory and learning 69, 73–8
Michener, James 62–4
Miller, Shawn, *Blueberry Hermit
Crab (Coenobita purpureus) in
Plastic Cap 127*
Mobius, Karl 90
moulting 14–15, 22, 81–4, *82,
83,* 128
mukbang 122–4

Orkin, Otto 38

pain and suffering 69–73
Peeters, Clara, *Still-life with Crab
106*

Philo of Alexandria 111
Poindexter, Oriana
*Brown Box Crab, Long Beach
102*
Rock Crab 68
pubic lice (*Pthiris pubis*) 17–18

Queen Crab 64

Rathbun, Mary Jane 28–9, 32–9,
53
Rathbun, Richard 28, 32–3
reproduction stages 13–14, *15,* 77,
77, 130–31
Richardson, Harriet 33
Rogers, Tanya L., *Callinectes
sapidus* (Atlantic blue crab) *76*
Roudez, Ross T. 75–7
Rouse, Greg 41, 42, 52

Sagan, Carl 66–7
Sartre, Jean-Paul 7–8
Schenck, Hubert G. 34
Schmitt, Waldo L. 33–4, *33, 37,* 38
Schnytzer, Yisrael 91–4
Scripps Institution of
Oceanography 41, 52, 81
Sebastian the Crab (in Disney's
The Little Mermaid) 60–61, 67
Seid, Charlotte
*Armed Box Crab (Playmera
gaudichaudii) 124*
Coconut Crab (Birgus latro) 10
*Pacific Sand Crab (Emerta
analoga)* 10

White-spotted Hermit Crab
(*Dardanus megistos*) 26
Shakespeare, William 55
shellfish poisoning 105, 113
Simonson, Lily, *Kiwa Puravida 43*
Smith, Steve 133
Smithsonian Institution 28, 32–4,
37–8, *49*
Stachowicz, John 96
Stevens, H. C. 95–6, 99
surimi 114–15

Taylor, Jennifer 81–3
Thurber, Andrew 41–2
tool use 88–9
Tyler, Paul 42

Valerio, Manuel 34
Van Gogh, Vincent 106, 108
Two Crabs 109
Vernygora, Oksana 51
Verrill, Addison 33

Walter, Robert C. 104
Warner, William 56, 117
Withers, Thomas Henry 21
Woods Hole Oceanographic
Institution 52

Zoidberg, Dr John (in *Futurama*)
61